W9-AVR-827

Letters to Myself on Dying

for our children

Letters to Myself on Dying

A Journal of Hope, Pain, and Courage

MIRTH VOS

A Division of Baker Book House Co
Grand Rapids, Michigan 49516

and

CRC PUBLICATIONS

2850 Kalamazoo SE
Grand Rapids, MI 49560

Published by Baker Books
a division of Baker Book House Company
P.O. Box 6287, Grand Rapids, MI 49516-6287

and

CRC Publications
2850 Kalamazoo SE
Grand Rapids, MI 49560

Printed in the United States of America

Library of Congress Cataloging-in-Publication Data

Vos, Mirth, 1937–
Letters to myself on dying : a journal of hope, pain, and courage / Mirth Vos.
p. cm.
ISBN 0-8010-1189-2 (Baker Books).—ISBN 1-56212-456-0 (CRC Publications)
1. Cancer—Patients—Religious life. 2. Vos, Mirth, 1937– Diaries. 3. Cancer—Patients—Canada Diaries. I. Title.
BV4910.33.V67 1999
248.8'6196994'092—dc21
[B] 99-16359

For current information about all releases from Baker Book House, visit our web site:

http://www.bakerbooks.com

Introduction

Who is "myself"? I am a middle-aged, middle-class, Caucasian North American woman who is fighting cancer. Cancer has reared its cobra head over my life three times: in 1982, in 1990, and in 1996. Its last strike—breast cancer in the lungs—will (almost certainly) take my life, although three years have passed since the diagnosis.

I went to university and married within the calm certainties of the fifties. With little soul-searching, my husband and myself produced four children in quick succession. The winds of the sixties and seventies shook us as they did everyone else, especially through the challenges given us by our teenagers. By 1982, my husband was ending a long pastorate in Toronto. By 1982, I had been emotionally freed up through psychotherapy, and, to my own astonishment, had reached the goal of becoming a psychotherapist. For years I had thought I would be a writer.

At this time an ovarian cyst announced itself through sudden, blazing pain. In the middle of a doctors' strike I had immediate surgery. Six weeks later I submitted to a radical hysterectomy, the preventive treatment prescribed at that time for one who has had an ovarian cyst that shows "low-grade malignancy." I hid in that term, avoiding the cancer word whenever I could.

A sidebar to my health history has been the onset of depression whenever my body lacks sufficient estrogen. The effect of the radical hysterectomy was devastating. Despite the excitement and satisfaction of moving to a new community and joining three partners in a counselling practice, my inner world was pervasively bleak. The naturopathic drops that I tried did not help.

After two years, my cancer specialists looked at their research stats and decided that the type of cyst I had had was not one nourished by estrogen. They judged that a person with my history had no greater chance of developing cancer again than one who had not had such a cyst. They prescribed estrogen for me, and—my energetic, cheerful self came back! I trusted these experts and veiled from myself the concerns about estrogen that were being raised in the media. I couldn't face living without it.

I believe now that the estrogen is the reason for my subsequent cancers. My doctors routinely demur when I say that, and who will ever know? What followed as I used it were six years of life at its richest—productive work, family joy, innovative leadership within my church.

In 1990, shortly after a negative mammogram, I experienced what a woman fears most: the discovery of a breast lump. This time, a radical mastectomy. For two weeks I was distraught with fear and grief; then equilibrium returned. Because five years after their illness, 78 percent of women have recovered from breast cancer, right? My nodes and bones and liver were clear; there was no reason to believe that anything but complete recovery lay ahead for me. I had six months of chemotherapy as "insurance" and returned to my demanding, satisfying life routines. No estrogen now, of course (six more years of data, now devastating), so my old enemy depression pounced again. This time an antidepressant was prescribed.

Meanwhile I exercised and abjured fat and sugar. Ingested fiber and betacarotene in every form. Read books about cancer and took many supplements. Survived, my survival of three years coinciding with the tenth anniversary of my being in private practice. My husband and I gave a party to celebrate this double blessing. But when we moved to a new pastorate, I did not divulge my cancer history to new friends.

Then the shattering third diagnosis. I had misunderstood that statistic about the 78 percent survival. It is not that one is in the clear *after* five years. *The five years are* the survival period. One remains a positive statistic, but cancer often returns after that. In my case six years had passed. In its new form the disease was not curable, only fightable.

I pitched forward into grief. Faith issues battered me. I prescribed journaling for myself, a healing technique often used in psychotherapy. For a year I punched in the entries; and then, as almost always happens with journaling, a significant change occurred. This should not have surprised me, but it did.

Many of us walk the road of an incurable disease. Many of us walk beside a person who is on such a road. Our jumbled sequences of grief and faith differ. I offer my journal to encourage each person to go to the depths of what she or he is experiencing, with honesty and without fear.

> Therefore we do not lose heart. Though outwardly we are wasting away, yet inwardly we are being renewed day by day.
>
> 2 Corinthians 4:16

April 1999

Monday, April 22 I walk up the stairs from my lower level office, echoes of the last psychotherapy session with a client fading with each step.

My inner world shifts to "cooking mode," finding within it a pool of expectation, the commonplace joy of a shared meal. I reach the top; in sync Jack's figure emerges from the hall. Instantaneous shift—red alert—the quietness in his face. Body and brain pull back.

"Dr. Stanford called a few minutes ago, wanting to know when he could speak to you personally about the results of the CAT scan."

I instantly know why the personal contact, as Jack has known just before.

The call is almost immediate: the doctor's quiet voice telling me that five spots of cancer are present in my lungs and chest wall, I writing the data down, his stilled voice saying that this is serious indeed, saying that he is so very sorry, I thanking him with dignity, I breaking down only when he says that he will be praying for Jack and me and that an oncologist's appointment has been made.

And so the world as we know it tumbles into free fall. Like detritus from a spaceship, our love and our future spiral downward through a limitless darkness of time and timelessness. The renovated kitchen and the awakening yard through its window tilt crazily into a different configuration, the harmonious spaces we created for each other mocking us with their transience, their fixedness for the moment, their imminent departure; there is an instant stupid thing-ness about them now that a moment/aeon before I had eagerly grasped as valuable.

We cling to each other, the first of embraces irrevocably changed. I am poised at the beginning of a path leading away from him; he is standing still, firmly fixed in this life. This rending from each other claws us apart even as our bodies sway in the motions of oneness, in-the-same-place-ness. We search each other's contorted face. Hot tears screech from our eyes. What was is over. A new phase—our final phase—catches us in an entangling net. Other couples may be living this stage without knowing it; we know.

The knowledge—not present to us only a moment ago—now sits in our face, waits. It is squat and ugly, like a lumbering wheelbarrow to be balanced and maneuvered through these rooms, through tonight, through days, through crowds, through everything. About fifteen minutes have passed.

For my days vanish like smoke; my bones burn like glowing embers. . . . My days are like the evening shadow; I wither away like grass.

Psalm 102:3, 11

Tuesday, April 23 We are packing to drive the hour north to a resort for a pastor couples' retreat.

The night has been like none other in our experience. Millions know this night; we are new inductees. Quite a number of friends, some members of our extended families, and many congregation members and clients have entered this room before us, a room in which thoughts and visions ricochet off the walls and batter the bereft person with an overstimulation of pain.

In overdrive, the brain makes connections with lightning speed, creating searing awarenesses, discharging its energy through sobbing that chokes off breath. The sinuses fill; I blow my nose loudly and repeatedly, humbled by my body's crudeness. In the pinched register of cry-talk we decipher the scenes flashing before us: He sees the hospital bed in the dining room; I see him sitting beside it, his head against my body, communing with me when I am too weak to respond. We see our children.

Exhausted after several hours, we halve a sleeping pill and share it like a sacrament.

We say to each other, "God is here with us. He loves us."

> *Hear my voice when I call, O LORD; be merciful to me and answer me. My heart says of you, "Seek his face!" Your face, LORD, I will seek.*
>
> Psalm 27:7–8

WEDNESDAY, APRIL 24 Today, once with colleagues at the retreat house, our friendly selves come out. The scheduled presentation "Change in the Family" is engaging. Only singing is intolerable; the diaphragm muscles used for singing are the same that stretch to sob. Several times we are directed to sing a song with many lines about trusting God with the future. I white-knuckle it, clenching my teeth, willing the tears to fall back into the secrecy of my lower lids. Jack is fighting the same fight.

At night we reenter the room of anguish.

Record my lament; list my tears on your scroll—are they not in your record?

Psalm 56:8

Thursday, April 25 A young couple is at the retreat—two persons with whom we have many ties. We both feel a strong longing: We want to tell them our situation. Since I have had cancer before—a mastectomy six years ago—we know the process of one's becoming a cancer patient in people's eyes, of bearing the anxiety and the concern of many, especially of psychotherapy clients. So, in our nights of pain, we have already decided to keep what is happening to ourselves until chemotherapy is prescribed. Why now this urgency to tell? Why would we burden these two persons with grief, then ask them to share it with no one else?

I stay in our room until mid-morning. Jack returns to find out whether I am ready to take on the public. "I told them," he blurts.

A shock of fear, excitement, and relief.

"They were horrified. She simply put her arms around me."

Yes. That is it, isn't it? That shiver, the heartbreak in their faces—it has to be there, honoring the bond we four have, as we feel compelled to honor them with our extremity. Not showing them what lies beneath our cheerful facade would be betrayal. Our urgent drive to be authentic is simply—love. We love them. We trust their love for us.

On a chest in our living room stands a foot-high forged sculpture by Canadian artist Richard Kremer, given to us by these friends. When red-hot, its steel was pulled into two elongated figures, one taller, whose burnished planes turn slightly toward each other as the "faces" look outward. The upward sweep and downward stroke shaping the lovers create a sinuous sweetness from the cool bronze-black metal. The concluding sentence of our friends' note with the sculpture had said, "Thank you for what you have shown us as a couple."

These persons *see* us, and we are impelled to have them look into our cauldron of pain.

I remember the Lord Jesus asking his friends to be with him in his fear. I never knew before how much he loved Peter, James, and John—sometimes he must have felt *seen* by them, despite the denseness of their understanding. He takes them into the deeper shadows of the olive grove; he comes back twice; he tries to rouse them. How human this urgency, this need to be seen in his suffering, his need to have them watch and pray! In naivete and exhaustion, they fail.

But we will never need to rouse him, because he is watching, through all the hours. He is the one who over time has pulled our partnership into strength and sweetness. In the garden with us now, he witnesses our desperation. With sight far clearer than that of any friend, he *sees*.

He forges us still.

He took Peter, James and John along with him, and he began to be deeply distressed and troubled. "My soul is overwhelmed with sorrow to the point of death," he said to them. "Stay here and keep watch."

Mark 14:33-34

Monday, April 29 We meet the oncologist today. I have seen her before; she has done my checkups since we moved to this city.

The institutional waiting room physically holds us, but we are suspended in time. We dressed, drove, and ascended to this eighth floor, holding time away from us by silence and quiet movements. The two women in the reception cubicle are friendly and smiling; the over-long valances at the windows scream cheer. We grapple time down, pretending that we are not breathing.

But. My name is called.

I know this narrow room: Here four months ago she had delighted in my good health, suggesting that I was so well they could fit my routine check in anytime, suggesting that her department call me instead of my making the usual six-month appointment. Today her beautiful East Indian face is steeled.

"There are five spots of cancer on your lungs." She points to the scan and gives their dimensions in millimeters. The largest is the size of a dime. "This is incurable. But we will make you comfortable."

Jack's eyes lose their focus, the skin of his face empties out. I see myself drawing my feet up into the bed like the patriarch Jacob and, unlike Jacob, being handed the requisite morphine. We bow invisibly beneath the sentence, held upright by a carapace of dignity. But my insides swoon, and his gaze smears. She says an estrogen blocker, Tamoxifen, will be tried first to stop the growth of the tumors, and after that, chemotherapy, if the blocker is not effective.

Then, Jack, who knows my body better than I know it myself, honors the formality of leaving the room so that the doctor can examine me. She asks, "Is there anything you want to say while he is not here?"

Startle reflex. For days I ponder what situation could prompt this question from a professional who often takes part in others' tragedies. She uses it like the second question of a form, so it must have its place. To me, it is as if she is suddenly asking whether I like curry, or what is the balance on my Visa card. It is incomprehensible. *Is there anything you want to say while he is not here?* What might that be . . . for someone else? Doesn't she know that it is only by sagging into each other and marching in lock-step that we have been able to come here at all?

The fact that some, perhaps many, cancer patients face their disease in emotional separateness from their partners opens its chasm before me. I jerk back from it to follow the intelligent hands that are probing my scarred chest . . . neck . . . armpit. She asks about pain and I admit to aching twinges of it. She will immediately arrange for five consecutive radiation treatments at the Toronto cancer hospital to lessen the pain.

I flounder questions. How long? She cannot say. She says no one recovers from cancer that has spread this much. "We fight it with everything we have, but it always outwits us."

She touches my shoulder with a gesture that seems involuntary, her head slightly bent. Perhaps it is a salute to my devastation, or to some measure of gallantry that I am showing. With soft but firm diffidence she says, "I will be with you." She means this to be a comforting pledge.

In my rage I am ungrateful. What a rotten job. What a rotten job.

In our home we walk from room to room, meeting, holding, crying.

"I feel that I am going on a long journey and that I am already waving good-bye."

"You are."

A phrase clangs in my mind: *"Put your money where your mouth is."* Like a gong. "Mirth, you're so interested in spirituality, in meditating, in teaching others spiritual disciplines . . . well, now you are going to know God fully; you will see him 'face-to-face'; you're going to live in perfect communion with God. Do you have faith or don't you? [Clang.] This is what you believe; you've lived by this belief and now it's being fulfilled . . . respond, woman! PUT YOUR MONEY WHERE YOUR MOUTH IS. [Clang, clang.] Why these squawks of protest? This hanging back? This is the test, this is IT, what you've professed, what you've confessed, it's here, in front of you, time to walk the talk, live the talk you've talked . . . are you for real or not?"

Loud. I'm blinking tears. Assaulted by the clangs of awareness. Agreeing. Yes. I've happily lived a blueprint faith, which is now demanding its building. I didn't *know* that it was a blueprint until this moment, when I notice that I am shuddering at how concrete it must become. I am not ready, I cannot adjust. It's too big, too total, it's too much God. I cannot handle that much God. "Depart from me, for I am a sinful woman."

> When Simon Peter saw this, he fell at Jesus' knees and said, "Go away from me, Lord; I am a sinful man!" For he and all his companions were astonished at the catch of fish they had taken.
>
> Luke 5:8–9

On the weekend we have planned to celebrate several family birthdays. Now we sob to each other that we cannot wait. While not giving the reason, Jack's breaking voice communicates emergency as he phones our children. Of the six, which includes two partners, four can come that evening. And . . . I now remember: I've scheduled a psychotherapy session for after dinner. I must locate some composure.

When a few more minutes of that session are left, I hear their muffled entry upstairs, voices indistinct. I assume they have been told as I walk up to join them. But they are pass-timing about driving and the weather; flushed and awkward, they wait. I wail, grieving their tension; wail, ending it: "I have cancer again, and this time it is not curable."

"I knew it had to be that." Said with tiredness. Anyone. Grief already digging its jagged spaces.

We tell them the sequence. Mid-February, tiny beeper-like pains along the breastbone, once in a while, usually not present, but then again returning. The family doctor's reassurances, the X ray just to make sure. The X ray repeated: There is a puzzling "something"; the fluoroscopy in early March, "not quite clear." Two weeks ago, the CAT scan. The family doctor's call. The finality of the oncologist's labelling.

I say things. With the top of my brain I take truths off the shelves of my faith storehouse: "I am in a good place spiritually. I'm glad I have my discipline of daily devotions, of meditation, to use, to keep me close to God." "I will be okay; it is thinking about all of you without me that I cannot bear." "This is a new time now, for us as a family. There will be good things about it, just as we have had many good things before." One of them watches me warily, as if I am a specimen never before seen.

I sit by each one, touch them, cry, and tell them how much I love them.

We inhale the familiar room. The familiar objects in their places. The familiar persons so widely disparate in temperament, impulses, experiences, goals. A family. With a family's brave and plodding history, relationships spattered by hurt but also sparkled with joy. Like the sofa and the pictures, we expect one another, too, each to be there "in place," so that we *each* can feel in place in *our* places. But now we are all awry; this is not our usual crisp affectionate casual, this is breathy and soft, each figure mushed around the edges.

Each of us is seeing the circle broken. Each of us sees the circle re-forming. It is smaller by one link. It is still linked and strong.

As a father has compassion on his children, so the LORD has compassion on those who fear him; for he knows how we are formed, he remembers that we are dust. As for man, his days are like grass, he flourishes like a flower of the field; the wind blows over it and it is gone, and its place remembers it no more. But from everlasting to everlasting the LORD's love is with those who fear him, and his righteousness with their children's children—with those who keep his covenant and remember to obey his precepts.

Psalm 103:13–18

TUESDAY, APRIL 30 Today our fourth child and her partner come. She rushes up the flagstone walk, her face flushed with crying, her eyes leaping the distance between us, drenching me with love.

We share a meal, the bread of tears. Once or twice we laugh hysterically.

Anyone who loves his father or mother more than me is not worthy of me; anyone who loves his son or daughter more than me is not worthy of me; and anyone who does not take his cross and follow me is not worthy of me. Whoever finds his life shall lose it, and whoever loses his life for my sake will find it.

Matthew 10:37–39

Friday, May 10 These days I am frantically scrambling through the Bible, like a mother whose child suddenly gets lost in a crowd. My eyes burrow down into the pages and at the same time dart up and down the columns, pleading for words that speak to my plight, begging balm for my lacerated gut. Whenever I find them, I write them out on strips of paper that now seem to be available just for this use. How strange that as I face my end I use the final remnants of a huge cache of papers that Jack bought at an industrial auction long ago, leftover pieces from legal-sized sheets that we have been cutting to letter size.

These strips now drop into my need, white pieces turning into manna when I write on them the verses for which I am starving. Examples:

> *Therefore everyone who hears these words of mine and puts them into practice is like a wise man who built his house on the rock. The rain came down, the streams rose, and the winds blew and beat against that house; yet it did not fall, because it had its foundation on the rock.*
>
> Matthew 7:24–25

and

> *And we rejoice in the hope of the glory of God. Not only so, but we also rejoice in our sufferings, because we know that suffering produces perseverance; perseverance, character; and character, hope. And hope does not disappoint us, because God has poured out his love into our hearts by the Holy Spirit, whom he has given us.*
>
> Romans 5:2–5

and my favorite right now,

> *But you, dear friends, build yourselves up in your most holy faith and pray in the Holy Spirit. Keep yourselves in God's love as you wait for the mercy of our Lord Jesus Christ to bring you to eternal life.*
>
> Jude 20–21

The areas where I work are now drifted with manna—the sill above the kitchen sink; the ledge by the NordicTrack™ where I exercise; my desk drawer. *He humbled you, causing you to hunger and then feeding you with manna, which neither you nor your fathers had known, to teach you that man does not live on bread alone but on every word that comes from the mouth of the* LORD *(Deut. 8:3)*. Between clients I pull the drawer out to look at the verses spread within it, in this way anchoring my own extremity while preparing to once again enter another person's broken world. *Fix these words of mine in your hearts and minds; tie them as symbols on your hands and bind them on your foreheads (Deut. 11:18).*

> For everything that was written in the past was written to teach us, so that through endurance and the encouragement of the Scriptures we might have hope.
>
> Romans 15:4

What am I doing? My brain is trying to burn God's reality into itself, to balance out the death reality that makes me shriek. Because levels of my consciousness clash against each other with competing thoughts: (1) Instead of being with your partner you will be seeing God face-to-face—what a terribly cruel either/or! and (2) Never let go of God's love for you, a love far beyond human love.

> Now what I am commanding you today is not too difficult for you or beyond your reach. It is not up in heaven, so that you have to ask, "Who will ascend into heaven to get it and proclaim it to us so we may obey it?" Nor is it beyond the sea, so that you have to ask, "Who will cross the sea to get it and proclaim it to us so we may obey it?" No, the word is very near you; it is in your mouth and in your heart so that you may obey it.
>
> Deuteronomy 30:11–14

An article by J. I. Packer in a recent issue of *Christianity Today* says that the Bible is a lifeline that offers the possibility of safety to a person who is drowning. Before, I read the metaphor as commonplace, even hackneyed. Before, I had not known drowning. But now I *am* drowning, spiraling downward, flailing about, then surfacing, gulping air. I gulp Bible truth—God's love, God's presence, the Spirit praying for me, Jesus' personal willingness to suffer, his resurrection, the glory that waits—and I do feel safe. But my lungs still gurgle water—a yell of protest. I am confused that years of living the faith have not created in me an eagerness to leave this life and be with the Lord.

Deep calls to deep in the roar of your waterfalls;
all your waves and breakers have swept over me.

Psalm 42:7

I *have* often voiced a longing for the new heaven and earth when wearied by the evil hidden for years that clients tell me about in my practice . . . when corruption in public life is once again exposed . . . when I cannot escape the TV pictures of massacres and famine. Yes, I often have comforted myself by anticipating a new heaven and earth. Has this just been a way of dissociating? I am not eager to flee this terrible world now! I want to live to be eighty, to care tenderly for my partner in his old age. I find this "terrible" world quite acceptable! It is my arrogance that is terrible: I feel cheated if I am not to have retirement years—my comfortable, Registered Retirement Savings Plan-supported, slowed-down years full of loving and being loved.

Yes, I am drowning.

And I am surfacing. I steep my day in Bible truth and cry every night.

And each night God shows me Peter walking on the waves to meet Jesus, his eyes locked into Jesus' gaze. The Spirit enables me, too, to see Jesus, to step out of the boat, and to walk toward him on the treacherous water, eyes not leaving his. My spluttering and gasping stops.

Let us fix our eyes on Jesus, the author and perfecter of our faith, who for the joy set before him endured the cross, scorning its shame, and sat down at the right hand of the throne of God.

Hebrews 12:2

I will convulse again tomorrow. Behind my exterior composure of working with clients, attending a meeting, or talking on the phone. And I will grab the lifeline.

The cords of death entangled me, the torrents of destruction overwhelmed me. The cords of the grave coiled around me; the snares of death confronted me. In my distress I called to the LORD; I cried to my God for help. From his temple he heard my voice; my cry came before him, into his ears.

Psalm 18:4-6

TUESDAY, MAY 14 The radiation treatments are scheduled for five consecutive working days at the primary cancer hospital in Toronto. Driving there, we need silence. No music, although our habit is to use the car as our box for a private CD concert. Probably the computers of our minds are being taxed to the limits of their RAM. The hour-long prelude to the city works its rural peace; then we enter the kaleidoscopic energy—a stream of people and traffic in a wind tunnel of buildings and overpasses. May sunshine splatters everything; colors tumble and splotch. This serious trip is becoming an exhilarating outing!—but how ruefully weird that it is death in my lungs that carries us forward today into the city's exuberant life.

We find the new cancer hospital, a replacement for the one I went to for years for checkups after my 1982 surgery for an ovarian cyst. I miss its worn environment today. There, we patients sat in old, brightly lit waiting rooms, elbow to elbow and almost knee to knee. I and the other Caucasians tried to stretch the hospital's skimpy, worn, white terry gowns over our legs' awful whiteness, while members of the more beautifully toned races seemed not as challenged by the gowns, more decently clothed by their own skin. The communal *dishabille* was accented by assorted wigs' rigid perfection. (Of course, friends of patients sat among us in street clothes.) All conversations were overheard. Quite often gurneys bearing persons appearing to be very ill were wheeled through. Motherly types in smocks and lipstick steered trollies among the knees, offering juice, tea, coffee, and arrowroot biscuits. The best part of this scene for me were the issues of the *New Yorker* strewn among the magazines: I'd collect two or three, do the cartoons, and read the silky prose.

I liked these crowded clinic scenes; we were all being leveled down into the lame, the halt, the blind. Even more so than Florida, Princess Margaret Hospital was God's waiting room. Stupidly, I sometimes felt a little smug, being younger than most, having "only" a "low-grade" malignancy.

My time had not yet come.

My time has come. We circulate around the new Princess Margaret, which has vast areas positioned around a many-storied atrium spiralled with stairs and see-through elevators. The lighting is soft; fat chairs are pushed against the soaring outer walls. The large spaces create oases of separateness; the carpet and upholstery absorb conversation, making all exchanges private.

Very long wide halls lead to the departments where the actual treatment is given. One might see a gurney across a wide expanse, being pushed through doors into another wide hall. There are no trollies, no magazines. There is a wonderful deli and a magazine shop on the main floor, for heaven's sake.

We find the radiation department and meet the radiologist's nurse, who is dressed in a power suit. The radiologist is a stocky Scot—red-gold beard, burred speech. "So, you have these spots on your lungs. Some people live for months or a year and even years with such spots. The radiation may produce a flushed, rash-like area. Don't worry about that. Today my assistants will place small tattoos on your body to guide those who will be radiating you."

He has said something electrifying!

I notice that everyone meeting me looks up from their sheaf of files to ask my date of birth. The one tattooing me explains, "Persons are often anxious and confused and answer to any name. The birth date question is more trustworthy." Fascinating. In the cramped rooms of the old hospital, names rang out pretty clearly. This place is muffled like a temple.

In the car we interrupt each other, each saying, "Did you hear him say it? *Years!* He did say it, didn't he? That little *s* . . . ! He said it; he said it! *Years!*" Jack navigates the frightful traffic automatically, joining me in a daze of possibility. *He did say years!*

Hezekiah turned his face to the wall and prayed to the LORD, "Remember, O LORD, how I have walked before you faithfully and with wholehearted devotion and have done what is good in your eyes." And Hezekiah wept bitterly. Before Isaiah had left the middle court, the word of the LORD came to him: "Go back and tell Hezekiah, the leader of my people, 'This is what the LORD, the God of your father David, says: I have heard your prayer and seen your tears; I will heal you. On the third day from now you will go up to the temple of the LORD. I will add fifteen years to your life. . . .'"

2 Kings 20:2-6

TUESDAY, MAY 21 It is the day of the fifth and final radiation treatment. Jack is out of town, so I bus into the city. I sit in the high, plush seat among sullen and obstreperous, much-baggaged commuters and feel very calm and . . . coolly . . . dead. I am an alien, I am dying.

I view them all through a telescope, their buzz of ordinary life clear and distant.

From my work with grieving clients, I recognize this as the incomprehension of grief. How can people shoot about on their merry trajectories, puzzles the torn one . . . lorn one . . . shorn one. . . . There is all that life over there . . . it is just amazing how everything goes on . . . the animated faces . . . but I have no connection to it, frown even at the thought. I can go through the motions, of course; no one notices. But I am more attenuated than those people so far away, much colder, too; I am standing in the barrens, staring at their bright to and fro.

And so, too, the long subway ride. Ordinarily, the tapestry of races in the Toronto subway brings me joy. But *I am dying, I am dying, I am dying.* Remote.

I am amazed at the egocentricity of grief. Undoubtedly among these people are persons who have suffered devastations much worse than mine. Most of them may not know Christ. Perhaps some have had a child die, have had childhoods of parental abuse, have at this moment relatives in Bosnia or Chechnya for whom they fear the worst. Undoubtedly many have been scarred by relationships, made insecure or hard. A percentage of those riding the bus, swarming this subway, have chronic pain, an addiction, cancers. How strange that my trouble does not make me immediately identify with them, does not create compassionate love.

I know that grief is a psychological and physiological state with documented peculiarities. Its disorienting effect is as radical, although in a negative way, as the disorientation that occurs when one is falling in love. So I forgive myself my strange perspective and instruct my faith to form a correcting picture. It is of the Lord Jesus moving among crowds such as this, proceeding toward his death. No subways or buses with seat-boundaries, just jostling bodies vying for place, for touch, for toeholds of space within earshot of what he is saying. And he not placing himself apart but remaining accessible to their words and touches. Giving them in return his own.

I crave that touch for myself.

At once Jesus realized that power had gone out from him. He turned around in the crowd and asked, "Who touched my clothes?" "You see the people crowding against you," his disciples answered, "and yet you can ask, 'Who touched me?'" But Jesus kept looking around to see who had done it. Then the woman, knowing what had happened to her, came and fell at his feet and, trembling with fear, told him the whole truth. He said to her, "Daughter, your faith has healed you. Go in peace and be freed from your suffering."

Mark 5:30–34

But stronger than that longing is the intuition that throwing myself into entreaty will pitch me into frantic desperation. Why should I presume that I should be healed? I can name several persons whom I had considered indispensable to God's work—and he took them in the full tide of their service. How then should I presume? Everything within me tells me to accept the heavy hand of the Lord as it comes to me in an incurable illness.

Alone, under the lead apron, the machine doing its quick burn, I suddenly wonder about research into patients' differing grieving styles and these styles' effect on the course of their cancer. I ask the woman administering the radiation, and she decides persons in the social work department would know. She phones, and yes, I can see someone if I go right up.

I negotiate a labyrinth of floors and corridors and find the numbered office in Dentistry. The emotional aspect of cancer must not be too important, bitter thought. A pleasant Asian woman is seated at a desk in a tiny room, and I take the chair flush against the side of her desk. My own office is palatial compared to this. Now I am the client. I wonder how she is processing me.

I slowly ask my question . . .

Then uncontrollable tears as she asks the details of my situation. The answer to my question is that every case of cancer is different and that each person responds differently. She offers books and tapes and encourages me to "take charge" of my illness. I ask her how she sees me. She says she sees me as very angry, outraged. This surprises me, because what I am feeling seems to me to be choking, Grand Canyon–sized sadness. Finally she says, "You say that you are dying. But you are not dying. You have many months, perhaps years, to live. You have no knowledge of how long your life may continue. You may have cancer, but you are not dying. You are not dying. Dying is something very different."

This is why God has brought me here. I receive the pearl, thank her with appropriate cadence, gather up the books and tapes, and once again negotiate Dentistry.

I am not dying.

Shape up, lady.

One of the books I take home from the hospital's library is the Canadian Cancer Society's spiral-ringed publication listing alternative therapies (alternative, that is, to surgery, radiation, and chemotherapy). I quickly leaf through the pages of diets, concoctions, and regimens. A message over-arches all of them: None of these approaches has been substantiated by research. And a warning: A cancer patient is vulnerable, so do not be duped by quacks. Scientific studies have proven the positive value of only one alternative therapy—relaxation and visualization. Patients who relax through deep breathing and then visualize their immune system as consisting of active, positive entities (such as knights on white horses), attacking and demolishing the cancer cells, symbolized by negative symbols (such as dragons), live longer and have less cancer pain than those who do not.

Such imaging I can do, since I have taught many clients to rehearse needed outcomes through the use of deep relaxation paired with the visualizing of dynamic, positive images.

What symbols shall I now use for myself?

THURSDAY, MAY 23 The local Christian school grade eight class has asked me to say a few words at their graduation. They have chosen these Bible texts: "Have I not commanded you? Be strong and courageous. Do not be terrified; do not be discouraged, for the LORD your God will be with you wherever you go" (Josh. 1:9) and "But one thing I do: Forgetting what is behind and straining toward what is ahead, I press on toward the goal to win the prize for which God has called me heavenward in Christ Jesus" (Phil. 3:13–14).

I wrestle with it. Grade eight students looking ahead to attending a secular high school choose texts. Myself, an older person staring at terminal illness, seizes upon texts. Sometimes the same texts, picked to address different situations. All of us anxious about the next stage of our lives. They, launched into unfolding life. I, launched toward life's ending. I understand they have chosen these verses from a list of many possible verses. I cull verses out of intense need. What does God think of our grabbing onto verses like this, when we are anxious, when we are desperate?

As I shape the short address, I accept the gift God is giving me. He makes me think about Joshua, who has not been brought to my attention for years. Three times in four verses God says to him, "Be strong and courageous." Twice in nine verses he pledges, "I will be with you, I will never leave you or forsake you." Can these promises to a nation at a crucial choice point be extrapolated to teens'—my—concerns in May 1996? Joshua getting ready to fight pagan armies, the teens doing battle with an environment heavily influenced by a pagan media, and my body fighting killer cells? God, are you promising *us* as you promised Joshua?

It seems as if God says, "Yes. You *can* be courageous, because I am with *you.* I am the same God today as I was in Joshua's time. But notice my words about *how to live* with my words: 'Be careful to obey all the law my servant Moses gave you; do not turn from it to the right or to the left, that you may be successful wherever you go. Do not let this Book of the Law depart from your mouth; meditate on it day and night, so that you may be careful to do everything written in it. Then you will be prosperous and successful'" (Josh. 1:7–8).

Aaaah. God does describe the way he wants us to live with Bible verses. He expects believers to move from anxiety and desperation . . . to meditation.

Well then, there are Paul's remarks about pressing on toward the prize for which Christ has called him heavenward, on which to meditate. I suspect the teens didn't look at this verse too closely; what they may have mainly gotten from it is its *energy*, something like "keep going bravely forward." But that "being called heavenward to win the prize for which one has been called"—*I* may not read over it. I am balking at being called heavenward with all my might! I'm not interested in the prize! I'm running backwards, *remembering* all that is behind, intensely cherishing it!

I cry out, "O Paul, how did you do it? Perhaps because you didn't have a partner . . . you didn't have children. . . . Think of an ordinary love relationship, Paul . . . wouldn't you feel differently then?"

I see Paul looking at me, waiting for me to finish and then bursting forth, brushing aside what I've said. "Mirth, you are *crazy* to hold on so tightly. You have no idea what is waiting for us! It's love beyond this-life experience, relationships beyond our experience, joy and fulfillment beyond experience . . . it's being with *Christ!* You have no idea . . . you just have no idea."

> I know a man in Christ who fourteen years ago was caught up to the third heaven. Whether it was in the body or out of the body I do not know—God knows. And I know that this man—whether in the body or apart from the body I do not know, but God knows—was caught up to paradise. He heard inexpressible things, things that man is not permitted to tell.
>
> 2 Corinthians 12:2-4

Why then am I crying? My stubborn emotions keep protesting, "It's such a cruel choice!" God forgive me.

FRIDAY, MAY 24 I keep turning to Revelation 1. Day after day I read verses 17 and 18: "Do not be afraid. I am the First and the Last. I am the Living One; I was dead, and behold I am alive for ever and ever! And I hold the keys of death and Hades."

More than two years ago Jack and I came into possession of an audiotaped reading of the Book of Revelation. On it, special effects of trumpets, synthesizer, and organ heighten the scenes' apocalyptic drama. Persons with differently timbered voices read the words of John, of the angels, and of the voice from the throne; massed voices chant the songs of the twenty-four elders and of the multitude without number.

At that time the fearful majesty of this tape repeatedly poured into our kitchen and into our car. I found that I had to prepare myself for listening to it; the presentation so shattered the immediacy of the mundane that to turn it on casually seemed to edge toward blasphemy.

For table devotions we also made use of two paperback copies of a commentary on Revelation, reading from them to each other, turn about, in conjunction with the tape. This immersion in Revelation left me with great joy. Up until then, ignorant as I was about apocalyptic literature, I had always turned away from Revelation's fantastic creatures and its cast of thousands. But the Holy Spirit used this informal daily study to bless me with a lively apprehension of the radiant beauty of God. My prayers began to frequently address God as Alpha and Omega, and for meditation I could hold in my inner vision the throne scenes of worship.

So—seeing the glorified Lamb is now my equation with dying. And his glory is what is making this death sentence so hard! I am oppressed; I feel strongly that I am not ready for the beatific vision. How strange my spiritual life is—I have conscientiously spent time in God's presence, have been nourished by it—and used that nourishment to turn to everyday life with zest. And now when there is a fork in the road—a turn leading directly to God—instantaneously, fiercely, I want more of the earthly-life road, not life in God's presence.

The glorified Son of Man says, "Do not be afraid." But I cry out that I cannot handle what lies ahead for me. "Do not be afraid." "Do not be afraid." "Do not be afraid." I am not really *afraid*. I am not *ready*.

> And when I turned I saw seven golden lampstands, and among the lampstands was someone "like a son of man," dressed in a robe reaching down to his feet and with a golden sash around his chest. His head and hair were white like wool, as white as snow, and his eyes were like blazing fire. His feet were like bronze glowing in a furnace, and his voice was like the sound of rushing waters. In his right hand he held seven stars, and out of his mouth came a sharp double-edged sword. His face was like the sun shining in all its brilliance.
>
> When I saw him, I fell at his feet as though dead. Then he placed his right hand on me and said, "Do not be afraid. I am the First and Last. I am the Living One; I was dead, and behold I am alive for ever and ever! And I hold the keys of death and Hades."
>
> Revelation 1:12–18

Saturday, May 25 A women's conference in the town where I used to live. Because it has drawn women from all over Ontario, most of them I do not know, but many of them I do know. I talk and smile. But I am not *in* my talk and smile; that now-familiar apartness imprisons me, turning the socialness I usually cherish into protocol. A leaden protocol. I am irritated by the presence of young children, for whom a nursery has been provided, but who are allowed to be brought to their mothers for differing reasons. I am appalled at myself; I am *for* the accessibility of small children to their mothers in various venues. The workshop I present does not go smoothly; the subject is controversial and only the first of four parts I had planned actually happens.

After it, a former client of mine, who is from a different theological tradition and who comes to my workshop just to have contact with me, said, "Well! I didn't know that you were such a Bible-thumper!" I have to agree, "Yes, that is what I am."

But . . . my emotions are not in sync with the thumping.

MONDAY, MAY 27 Each day becomes more bleak than the last. Yesterday I felt great anxiety about having adequate time to write what I wished to say to my children, as well as time to keep a record of what I am experiencing during this ending time of my life. I am becoming sure that I must stop seeing clients. Balancing my spiritual struggle with their recovery struggles is too hard. I can't keep it all straight. I feel it would be easier to die now and get it over with.

It is Jack who catches on. The Tamoxifen is causing my depression, as it did in 1990 when I had to stop taking it because of the profound depression it caused then. At that time I had had surgery and chemo and was cancer-free, so my oncologist approved my not taking it. But now I cannot stop this medication. Cancer is alive in my lungs.

To balance out Tamoxifen's effect, my family doctor prescribes the maximum dosage of an antidepressant.

New rage: Why wasn't that done in 1990? I could have continued with the Tamoxifen then, and perhaps the cancer would not have recurred! Impotent rage, shaking my fist at the medical world, and especially at myself, for not thinking of that solution then. Gnashing my teeth. Why did no one think of an antidepressant, so that I could have taken the Tamoxifen? And I a psychotherapist!

I begin to make sense of it. That time period was before the introduction of the "clean" tricyclic antidepressants, before their common use as part of medical treatment strategies.

I calm myself by remembering that my life span has been determined by God. The brokenness of the created world touches everyone; why this tantrum that it touches me? Canadian news media frequently describe the situation of more than a thousand hemophiliacs who have contracted AIDS through transfusions of tainted blood not screened by the Canadian Red Cross. Many of their marriage partners have also been infected. How do they handle *their* rage?

Shape up, lady!

> *All the days ordained for me were written in your book before one of them came to be.*
>
> Psalm 139:16

> *Man's days are determined; you have decreed the number of his months and have set limits he cannot exceed.*
>
> Job 14:5

Wednesday, May 29 Today I experienced a dramatic lifting of spirits because of the increased antidepressant.

Today the ability to hold in my hand each small section of time—even a fifteen-minute globe of it—returned. Time had its brightness back. Time had a purpose back: my giving to Jack an expanded and deepened experience of being loved by me. Time had its freight of blessings back, its backlog of wonders and worthwhileness. The efforts of my life had their modest but clear shine of value again. Six sessions with clients who worked their way to new small freedoms, to the next risks, brought its familiar spent exhilaration. I prepared dinner with contentment.

Tears come quickly when I look ahead to telling brothers and sisters and mother about the tragedy that has begun: my being taken away from Jack's retirement years, from his old age. I scream against the relentless onset of our parting, this allotment of sorrow, our portion of broken life. We want to hold each other forever; I want that more than the joy of perfect fellowship with the Christ, the Father, the Spirit. I cannot believe the terribleness of the rending of each of us from the other. My faith stands apart, looking at me quizzically. It is real faith—*and*—I hate this real life situation. The real faith does not touch the chasm of grief chawing me in two.

My faith is dogged. It keeps loping behind me, close. "The righteous will live by faith" (Rom. 1:17). I will keep living even as I am dying. My helpless anger at this ripping away of my presence from Jack hurls itself at God, in whom I have faith. Scream. Hurl. Cry.

Though he slay me, yet will I hope in him.

Job 13:15

Thursday, May 30 This day had as its last section a meeting of the women's abuse recovery group that I have been leading for three months. The video we watched was about the spiritual damage suffered by a survivor who is surrounded by religious lies.

I sat divided into two parts—hearing the women's cries, dully probing inside myself for my own tragedy. My situation seems both simpler than theirs and totally other than theirs, cosmic. My situation is clean clear grief, and theirs is twisted torturous violation, exacting its daily price. My world is ending; and theirs, please, God, is opening up.

FRIDAY, MAY 31 The bone scan was done today. Depression was with me today. My driving around this pretty town mocked my dreams of having leisure here, biking at the waterfront, writing, having guests for weekends. The mockery was sour to my spirit.

Later I watered the newly planted flowers while Jack stained the deck. The beauty of the yard rips at our hearts; we share glances; we know what the other is thinking: "This is what we have been making to share with each other. But the 'each other' is coming to an end." We are both praying for time.

I was able to exercise today. As I used my NordicTrack™, my eyes saw the text I had laid on the window ledge, Jude 20 and 21: "But you, dear friends, build yourselves up in your most holy faith and pray in the Holy Spirit. Keep yourselves in God's love as you wait for the mercy of our Lord Jesus Christ to bring you to eternal life." The thought that it would be the Spirit who would keep me within the love of God relieved me: my self, my flesh is very weak. The depression turns my grief to bitterness and blots out God's love. But I believe that both Jack and myself are within God's love. I will plead for the Holy Spirit, I will plead to be filled with the Spirit. I will ask that I may value eternal life more. I will ask that eternal life be in my thoughts more, as it was when the death news first came. I will ask to be built up on the holy faith given to me.

June

Saturday, June 1 Yesterday Romans 1:17 helped me again: "For in the gospel a righteousness from God is revealed, a righteousness that is by faith from first to last, just as it is written: 'The righteous will live by faith.'" The thought came that this living with cancer that will not be cured is the last piece of life I will have to do *by faith.* After it, REALNESS. That carried me through the pieces of the day.

Today I careened from the cell leaders' breakfast meeting . . . to shopping "The Mile" . . . to talking on the phone . . . to vacuuming and cooking . . . to a wedding ceremony . . . to reading book reviews . . . to now.

The breakfast discussion among the faith cell group leaders led to our sharing reflections about our personal walk with God. Overall, we are looking for evidence of such a relationship with God in interactions with the members of our groups, and often we are disappointed. I encouraged the leaders to model such a spiritual walk and to talk forthrightly in their groups about their own spiritual selves. This looking together toward the fall season and to possible new faith cell groups, with these leaders who do not yet know my trial, carried me forward into ongoing life, as if the future stretched forward for the taking, the living. Momentum. Oddity to the feeling.

Later today I mentioned to someone close to me the possibility of family members wishing to confide in friends about my illness. Was it hard to guard my confidence? The answer: "No, we put it out of our minds and we go forward." What also was said was that knowing what is coming has a good aspect: We can purposefully enjoy every moment of the present. Listening, I felt the inexorable loneliness of my moments and hours, as I shunt about blocks of grief, moments of faith, heavy sets of perspectives, and searing surfaces through the long seconds of longer minutes.

Then I remember my own young blankness over against Jack's mother's dying—I never asked her about the process of bearing the illness of colon cancer, the exhaustion of preparing to meet God. She was as remote to me as a Bedouin woman. Though I saw her walk the gritty farm road after supper trying to churn a sluggish meal within her, she was as distant from me as a figure on a TV screen. I gave her nothing.

Later other family members' manner was the same: "We put it out of our minds and we go forward." I understand now: A person who is in the shadow of death, disease death, is there alone. What occupies me feverishly is to them an interlude of calm.

Jack brings his love to me over and over as we each are working through the day. A lingered kiss, a handclasp, his hand stroking my head. He feels much closer than God.

Yet it is God I am supposed to be loving. I am raging, really. All afternoon I sourly ached.

Tonight the thought came: "I'll just pretend that I don't have cancer. I'll drink tea and read the weekend newspaper book reviews and then putter through the small tasks of a Saturday night as I would six weeks ago—before death's shadow." And I did. I recognized that I had discovered one more option for the arranging of my mind—pretending.

My mind is frantic with rearranging.

Sunday, June 2 The worship service this morning put me in touch with transcendence, Jack being used by God to bring his truth to both our hearts. Because I had to announce the pre-service details, I was seated very close to the front, much closer to him, the preacher, than I usually am. Gladly I took notes as he spoke; looking downward I was shielded from the naked brilliance of the truth that hung a bridge between us.

The second half of John 14 was the sermon's content. Jack spoke of the frightful anxiety of the disciples, evoked by Jesus' speaking to them of his leaving. The word *anxiety* resonated through me. I recognized it to be an additional description of my state this last six weeks, as accurate as "grief." My confronting a shortened life span has brought me intense anxiety. Dissonance between my dream of being with Jack in the sweet rhythm of retirement, caring for one another as we age—a dissonance echoing from the tiniest to the most cavernous chamber of my mind. Anxiety. ANXIETY. Thoughts screeching to a halt, hurling themselves against brick.

So the disciples?

Jack spoke of a person's having the experience of entertaining certain kinds of guests, some who dragged the host family down, and others who brightened the atmosphere, causing the host family to wish they could stay always.

His description of the valued guest reminded me of words he uses between us when he describes my presence in his life: *stimulating, brightening*. He had wanted me to stay always. I worried a moment at the almost-tears in his voice; then firmness overrode the tremble. The disciples' not wanting Jesus to leave was because they loved him, he said. The question for the listeners to consider was whether they lived with Jesus that way, knowing him, loving him.

I have been living with Jesus that way for some time, looking at him and loving him by meditating on his words. But I love everything else, too. And it is I who am leaving, and I cannot send my spiritual self to live within my husband and children, comforting them by bathing them in my love. With my tiny creaturely mind my death casts itself into it that cruel either/or: total fellowship with Jesus—at the cost of ordinary communion with human beings whom I love passionately. Ah!, there's the rub. Even with the Holy Spirit in me, I love God passionately only in the tiniest of flashes, at which time his beauty is so fiery I cannot take it in for more than a few moments and turn with almost-relief to ordinary work and ordinary people.

The best part of the sermon was fastened to verses 21 and 23 of John 14: "Whoever has my commands and obeys them, he is the one who loves me. He who loves me will be loved by my Father, and I too will love him and show myself to him. . . . If anyone loves me, he will obey my teaching. My Father will love him, and we will come to him and make our home with him." I had a vision of God the Father and Jesus walking in the rooms of our home, being close by, hovering in the hallway, tenderly leading our thoughts and actions as we study, see clients, write, share meals. I have always experienced God's Spirit living within each of us individually, but the word *home* brought the Father and the Son to the physical home Jack and I share, which was a home of joy and which now is a home of joy and sorrow.

When anxiety was great within me, your consolation brought joy to my soul

Psalm 94:19

Writing this, the song "How Great Is the Love of the Father" offered its words to me:

How great is the love of the Father,
the love he has shown to us—
so great that he calls us his children,
and children of God we are,
and children of God we are!
What we are to be in the future
as yet has not been made known,
but when Christ returns, we shall see him,
and then we shall be like him,
and then we shall be like him.

Whatever does that mean: "and then we shall be like him"?

And we, who with unveiled faces all reflect the Lord's glory, are being transformed into his likeness with ever-increasing glory, which comes from the Lord, who is the Spirit.

2 Corinthians 3:18

WEDNESDAY, JUNE 5 Songs. Both Saturday at a wedding and before Sunday morning worship the participants were asked to sing "Love Divine, All Loves Excelling." Was

I the only one who noticed its words? While I require daily prayer and journaling just to get my thoughts lined up in the right way, just to make room for the Spirit's leading me in truth, these wedding guests and the Sunday families could belt out joyously,

Come, Almighty to deliver,
let us all thy life receive;
suddenly return, and never,
nevermore thy temples leave.
Thee we would be always blessing,
serve thee with thy hosts above,
pray and praise thee without ceasing,
glory in thy perfect love.

And,

Finish, then, thy new creation;
pure and spotless let us be;
let us see thy great salvation
perfectly restored in thee:
changed from glory into glory,
till in heaven we take our place,
till we cast our crowns before thee,
lost in wonder, love, and praise.

Typing it out, I recognize that this is a "maranatha" hymn, a "Come quickly, Lord" hymn. An individual is not singing about entering into the next life through death, but Christians are singing about the second coming. But I felt alone, singing it, distanced from everyone around me, because fairly soon I will be casting *my* crown before the Almighty. And I don't want to, yet. I want the "this is not going to happen for a long, long time" serenity of the audience admiring the beauty of the bride in her gown; I want the complacency of the Sunday congregation settling themselves in.

I grieve for myself, having to bear the intensity into which I am pitched by the words of songs. Suddenly a question from a corner of my mind: Would I rather that my life be snuffed out in a moment through an accident? "No!" all the rest of me shouts. This is better. I can get ready. I can intensify my love for my husband, my children. I can, through the Spirit within me, build myself upon the foundation of faith, keeping myself within the love of God. I have time. Praise God.

THURSDAY, JUNE 6 Jack told me his dream as we ate breakfast. He and I had been captured by members of a sect, and their intent was to subjugate us. We had made a pact together that we would fight against them with all our powers, physically as well as in other ways. In the second part of the dream he was alone but still fighting.

I took courage, knowing there is a fight ahead, and knowing he will survive my death. But because of tears I could not read Psalm 23, to which we had come in our table reading. Later as we held each other he said that when he was fighting alone he did not have the sense that he would not see me again.

Will we be together in heaven? To my finite mind, the known is so much better than the unknown. Faith teaches that the unknown, with God, is so much better than the known. My tiny skull rattles with the craziness of it, the twist.

Every day again, our grief must be emptied out like a bucket.

WEDNESDAY, JUNE 12 Six days have passed since I have tracked my wrestling with time and eternity.

Five days ago we received the good news that cancer has not spread to the bones or liver. We went to the appointment somewhat blank, braced. Hearing the oncologist speak the report felt to me as if I, on "death row," had received a pardon—at the very least, reprieve! How relative everything is, for we left feeling almost lighthearted, tumors as malignant as ever within me. The oncologist used the word *slow-growing* as a possible description of the cancer type; we would know at the end of June if the Tamoxifen was shrinking the spots and whether chemotherapy could be put off for a while.

In the patients' waiting area, I reread Dr. Carrington's short course for teaching cancer patients how to relax deeply and how to visualize their bodies' immune system destroying cancer cells. The imagery I have evolved is that of tiny angels (they can dance on the head of a pin, after all!) imbued with the explosive power of God Almighty, hurtling down upon the diseased areas and, starting from their edges, working to their center and annihilating them. Whenever I close my eyes, I visualize this destroying activity. The cancer cells are weak and stupid. They shrivel to wisps of nothing and vanish. Usually I fall asleep as this is happening, though I should stay alert and visualize purposively for a while. I instruct my unconscious to carry on the fierceness.

For he will command his angels concerning you to guard you in all your ways; they will lift you up on their hands, so that you will not strike your foot against a stone.

Psalm 91:11–12

So we breathe in and breathe out and go for the long haul. The Carrington material reminds me that my picturing being alive correlates with a better and longer outcome for me than my picturing scenes of dying. So now I am to be alive in this earthly sense. My mind dares—two years? four? I must get down and concentrate on staying alive. Lines from one of my own poems float:

> why these opening hands towards life?
> they've fondled dying, hypnotized;
> yet feet stride, lately paralyzed by pain.

I am to stride, living, towards death. Which is exactly what each person who is alive is doing, without the conscious knowing of it.

Am I fortunate that I know?

I overhear a member of the family finishing a sentence with ". . . when Mom is gone." The commonplaceness of the phrase stills me into cold rage, followed by inner shrieks of indignation. My family members are making an adjustment in their future, no doubt reluctantly, yet matter-of-factly. I see my life sinking with a slight ripple into the waters of existence, the opaque surface flattening out, the cleaved place gone.

I would speak the same if a loved one had a terminal illness.

With a shock I am prompted by the Holy Spirit to recall that this is what the Christian faith is all about! Death's swallowing swallowed up by life! My battered ego drags itself to the cross. It is hardly believable that God would be concerned about the well-being of such a self-preoccupied mite as I recognize myself to be. Unimaginable. I will surely have to be transformed to be able to be in the presence of the radiancy of God. I really dare not lift my eyes. Whining that my family will learn to live without me, when I will be perfected and welcomed into the presence of God! God, my tears are my shame, my repenting. I come to you without a single plea.

When the perishable has been clothed with the imperishable, and the mortal with immortality, then the saying that is written will come true: "Death has been swallowed up in victory. Where, O death, is your victory? Where, O death, is your sting?"

1 Corinthians 15:54–55

Thursday, June 13 Grade eight graduation tonight. My eyes widened: The girls were transformed into models, although the boys were still boys. I don't feel satisfied with my part; I think that, despite the energy of Joshua's courage and Paul's focused running, the talk was somewhat sober for a rah-rah graduation. Giving it, I looked at the auditorium of people, my faith community, and thought for a few seconds about what I must share with them eventually. But tonight I was still normal to them, not a cancer patient. Holding on to what is behind.

Afterwards, at home, Jack took a picure of me wearing my flowered dress. We are holding on to what is behind together.

Saturday, June 15 My bookshelf holds *The Art of Passing Over* by Francis Dorff. A few days ago I dipped into it, reading some paragraphs about "passing over" prayer. Whatever they said, I either gleaned from them or formulated because of their stimulation the insight that, whenever I am praying earnestly, I am practicing the art of "passing over," for I am in communion with God, which is the essence of my next existence. This comforts me greatly. With this insight I start to know how I am to do this striding forward in life, readying myself for death to this life. It is to be done in prayer, in sitting quietly, in gazing at the candle flame of the Holy Spirit, in crying out to God, in sinking into the realness of God, in looking at Jesus, in meditating on his ministry. If this continues to be part of my life, then I am getting ready. The rest of the time I can live into the goodness of this life with intensity. Is it that simple? My heart tells me it is simple.

I have been worrying about things too wonderful for me. Receiving the news of the cancer's return, my whole being seemed to leap ahead, trying to empty my self from all attachment, straining to love God with the purity my love will have when I have passed over. I can respect that response of myself. It did accomplish the breaking of the proprietary attitude I had towards my future. I had to give that future up, offering it as a sacrifice God was claiming. But trying to generate that perfect love was tearing me to inner shreds. My love haloed earthly people, earthly tasks, earthly colors, earthly views. I cried out, "I don't know how to do it!" I was stretched thin by painful anxiety. Now God is teaching me about passing over.

Most mornings I wake at seven, so there is time for the meditative praying. It seems that God wakes me, and I stagger into his presence. Shortly I am alert, and he speaks to me. I write out the conversations—my cries, the Father's reassurances.

When I have passed over, there will be no more cries. What will it be? What will . . . ? What . . . ?

My heart is not proud, O LORD, my eyes are not haughty; I do not concern myself with great matters or things too wonderful for me. But I have stilled and quieted my soul; like a weaned child with its mother, like a weaned child is my soul within me.

Psalm 131:1–2

Tuesday, June 18 Calm, despite darting thoughts throughout the day; weeping each night. I've been making telephone calls to my brothers and sisters. Jack hovers close while I speak my half of the conversation, my voice a thin whisper at the hard parts. Some cry out their horror, some are controlled, some pray and entreat God for a healing miracle. I feel ashamed of my knife news, cutting into each person's world.

Each agrees that withholding news of my illness from the community we serve is desirable in that it gives us some privacy-time. Several offer to come immediately, and I hold them back. "I'm well," I protest. "There will be time to come and see me when I am weak, confined to bed." As I speak, a year of time lengthens into distance, effortlessly elastic. I see days succeeding each other, routine following routine, projects accomplished. How pleasant it is, this vista, how charming! The shadow of death is just a faint smudge, almost out of sight.

The mind dupes itself with hope.

Sunday, June 23 The pain is increasing, sometimes stabbing, with an almost-sting to it. My reason tells me the Tamoxifen is not as effective as hoped and that chemotherapy will be started at the end of the month. Jack says he finds himself weeping at any moment that he lets himself think about our situation. The impact of death is like nothing I have experienced before—it is like being slammed against a wall over and over, arbitrarily, dully, stupidly. Both of us are accustomed to helping others, we are pro-active, problem-solvers, resourceful. Now we hold each other, dumb, helpless, fully aware. The implacability of what lies ahead makes me nauseous.

Jack preached this morning about "The Caring Shepherd." He said, "Let us stop for a moment and take in the deep concern God has for each of us. He focuses on each one of us with intense love." I believe, dear God, I believe. I want to wrap myself up in the reality of your love and distance myself from the factuality of illness, from human love's rending. But it is exactly *in* the illness, *in* the breaking that I need your love. Your love is not to blanket and smother me, it is to strengthen and temper me. Instead of escape I need perseverance, patient endurance.

Close persons today seemed to take our circumstances matter-of-factly. My loved one and I knew what each of us was feeling while it was happening, and later we acknowledged to each other that we felt abused by their manner. We are so raw that not to be seen in our flayed, pulp skin bewilders us. We are angry.

A call from someone tonight who has been close to many persons through the long travail of cancer illness and death. Relief, to speak about its craziness, its demands. To speak about the ungraspable, life with God. The friendship of joined prayers for a miracle—remission. Relief.

MONDY, JUNE 24 Many days, many shifts of thought. With my book club group I read Forrest Carter's *The Education of Little Tree,* written from the point of view of a Cherokee orphan who lives with his grandparents from the ages of six to eight. In its last chapters he tells of the deaths of his grandparents and of an elderly man, an important friend. The aboriginal faith in reincarnation causes the last words of both men to be a serene "It will be better next time." In her turn, the grandmother puts on a beautiful dress of dyed skins and waits alone in a rocking chair on her porch for her spirit to leave her. Coming up the path, the child sees her and realizes that she is no longer alive. These passings are as peaceful as leaves falling from a tree, an inexorable, gentle part of the life cycle.

I was startled that this childlike telling had the effect of bringing ease to my mind for a day or two. The words formed in my mind: "This is a normal process." The pulling apart of loved ones happens to everyone in a love relationship: Lovers lose their lovers, children lose their parents, parents sometimes lose children. No love relationship stops at the same time for both parties. It is natural that my spouse be a widower, that my grown children be motherless, that my grandchildren mourn a grandparent. For some it happens early, for some it happens later, for some it happens very late. For me and my family it is happening fairly early. It is a normal process.

My therapy work is a daily examination of process. The process of forming identity, the process of forming defenses, the process of re-deciding, the process of life energy caught, the process of life energy freed. The process of renewal, the process of rededication, the process of thriving. Process. This being snatched away from earthly love relationships is a normal process. The decay of my body as cancer assaults it is a normal process. It is the latter part of earthly life and it is normal. I must meet it with dignity, not with this outraged surprise, outraged protest.

So my thoughts for a few days. During this time I noticed that my dying soon or a bit later from cancer no longer seems unreal, a dream from which I shall wake. The "doubleness" of existence, when my mind telescoped every window view with a backdrop of eternity, is no longer happening either. The shadow of death is fully with me all the time and it is completely "other" from the details of everyday living. I can hold them in my mind at the same time. A dullness, a matter-of-factness has replaced the inner screaming of the first weeks. Several times I have become so absorbed in an activity that I have had an hour or more of actual forgetting!

Several activities I do without witnesses: my devotional life, my practice of psychotherapy. This living in the shadow of death is now another. No one around me quite understands; but, I would not have them understand. It is an understanding that must engage a person only when it cannot be escaped. This normal process is so abnormal that no one can grasp it vicariously. When the shadow takes a person in its talons, when one feels death's claws in one's back, that is time enough to understand. Why am I made lonely by my loved ones' sad eyes, their uttered compassions, their strong embraces? Because they are alive, and they expect to stay alive. I must give them the joy of that, I must celebrate their lack of threat in their place, for they do not even know about its lack. Between us a great gulf is fixed and, naming it now, I would not have it otherwise.

Jack's embrace is not part of the gulf. It is an almost defiant statement of now-ness, of is-ness, of we-ness, of time-ness. This is not over yet. We rest in it like babies, sensing each other's presence pouring into each other's pores. Each night we rest in it, after each night's tears. And each night we rest.

I will lie down and sleep in peace, for you alone, O LORD, make me dwell in safety.

Psalm 4:8

TUESDAY, JUNE 25 Today perhaps a hundred minister colleagues, spouses, and children gathered for an annual picnic at the shore-front home of a ministerial couple. The talk was of our church denomination righting itself after many years of yawing to and fro, talk of reconciliation, of kindness, of restructuring, of racial respect. Against this serious backdrop, the babies in our group evoked our wonder, the children darted in artless grace, and we adults sitting in a circle felt the soft breeze blowing from the water like the Spirit himself. The lake, wide. The boats, scudding like dancers under Chagall clouds in a firmament sky.

My inside scream came from my bowels: "I want to live!"

I am afflicted. That is my lot, and I wish to live it with patient endurance. And I will live, with God.

Hear my prayer, O LORD; let my cry for help come to you. Do not hide your face from me when I am in distress. Turn your ear to me; when I call, answer me quickly.

Psalm 102:1–2

SATURDAY, JUNE 29 Today a wedding took place between a man whose wife had died of cancer two years before and a woman widowed for many years. The officiating pastor was Jack, while I sat in a pew, a guest. Psalm 126:5—"Those who sow in tears will reap with songs of joy"—shaped much of the service: a song, the carefully chosen remarks of an adult child, and also the meditation. I was seated fairly close to the front; yet it seemed to me that I was watching a tableau taking place at a great distance. A surreal overlay was shadowing the event itself—my own children speaking of their happiness that joy had come back into the life of their father, my partner standing in the groom's place, a woman's blurred presence. Perhaps it was because he was already at the front, in charge and speaking about joy following mourning, that the now and future drama coalesced while I coolly watched from another planet. Words dull within me: "Yes, you must give him up; that is what this cancer is all about—giving your loved ones to other persons, who will then name the goodness of God and celebrate a return of happiness."

How puny I am, so mortal, so preoccupied with time sequences. I must give *that* up; I must trust God's timelessness, his always-ness, his seeing each person's life from beginning to end at the same time, his holding me and those I love most, carefully and with a father's love. I must step away from time and polish up what he tells me about eternity. I must stop arching time awareness over into that new event in my life, *forever-ness*. GIVE IT UP. I cry out to God for help.

> Let us then approach the throne of grace with confidence, so that we may receive mercy and find grace to help us in our time of need.
>
> Hebrews 4:16

MONDAY, JULY 8 We are on vacation. Our holiday is beginning with the long stretches of driving and riding that I love, music washing our vehicle wide, our attention continually pleased and diverted by towns and highway vistas. The goal is Cape Breton, Nova Scotia; getting there will take several days. We sit belted into well-designed seats, positioned close to each other in the midsized car, like pilot and copilot. The wordless synchronicity of an occasional exchanged smile, of hand on knee, or stroked cheek, cradles us.

This tender proximity, sustained over many hours, gives me joy with a sharp undertow of grief. My thoughts riff past vacations, some many years ago when our understanding of each other had painful gaps—noisy, economical vacations, car crammed with kids, camper crammed with stuff. Since then we have learned to pace our different temperaments to each other's comfort, we have grown in candor, and the generosity towards each other with which we began has turned into a wide-flowing gush of agape. The marriage has aged into excellence, like fine wine in an oak-lined cask, the cask of God's grace.

God, why are you ending it at its best?

I am taking eight Tylenol a day now to mask the pain that breathes with me.

I think of God designing marriage. I compliment him heartily: It is a splendid idea. I think of Jesus' first miracle enhancing a wedding. As I sit in the car, wondering if this is our last vacation, the aptness to our situation of the steward's surprised observation to the bridegroom at that wedding hits me: "You have saved the best for last!"

Jack's various sermons on Jesus' first miracle always emphasize the sign's luxurious, not-really-necessary aspect, in contrast with Jesus' healing miracles. The lavish stock of wine is performance art accessible to everyone. Its eloquence speaks of abundant life, quality life, life full of richness, and enjoyment flowing from the presence of Jesus. I have always loved this insight, because it has given me an exhilarating perspective for living, replacing the anxious moralism of my childhood. And I have tasted that wine, taste it right now.

Jack drives peacefully, expertly, not knowing my thoughts. "You have saved the best for last!" . . . Wait. Could "the best" be eternity? The life beyond the grave that I will be entering soon? But it cannot be "best" if this conjugal tenderness is not part of it, I rebel. It can't be best without that; if it doesn't include that, I don't want it.

In his mid-seventies, my father once remarked that the life he shared with my mother, now that they were elderly, was one of great pleasure doing everything together. I had responded, "It will be hard for you to be eventually parted." He smiled. "In heaven it will be that way with everybody."

I was astonished, knowing him to be an introverted, private person.

I *don't want* it to be with everybody. I want this, I want this, I scream, like a child clinging to his crib although his parents have placed a fine new bed in his room. I cognitively know that what is ahead will be "the best," but emotionally I still do not grasp or accept it. That deep undertow of pain. I imagine a new partner sitting in my place, and my mind spins seventeen ways, rebuking me for my hubris, asking God for forgiveness, relinquishing before him even the fantasy of control. But thoughts keep trailing in: That person too will be joining us in heaven. However will that work? I shudder with distaste.

> At the resurrection people will neither marry nor be given in marriage; they will be like the angels in heaven.
>
> Matthew 22:30

Tuesday, July 9 Driving for hours through successive towns has its charm; however, my illness now alerts me to what I haven't noticed since childhood trips: cemeteries. A sibling and I would play a "counting animals on our side of the road" game, with different species having different point values. However, if a cemetery occurred on one's side of the road, all the accumulated points would be wiped out. Now I notice that every town has a cemetery beside the highway; some have two. I feel that every forty-five minutes or so I am being hit while I am down. Because . . . my inner eye keeps seeing the cortege of my own burial procession, and closer in, family members and friends in that moment when the ritual has ended, when all turn away from the grave to walk back to their cars, some with an arm about another, others holding hands, subdued for a distance, then starting murmured conversations.

Whap whap. Miles of driving. I am getting pretty strung out. Grieving the ending of the marriage. Captivated by new sights. Flinching. Flinching again.

Wednesday, July 10 Last night before falling asleep I solved the problem of the cemeteries' assaults. No, God gave me this gift: "Mirth, don't identify with cemeteries. They really have nothing to do with you. *You* won't ever have to use a cemetery, unless someone close to you dies before you do. *You* will never be in one. The cemetery is just a convenience for those who have to do something with your empty-of-you body. A cemetery is a giant composter, really. Drain the poignancy, the drama out of cemeteries. They are just a convenience. *You* will be somewhere else—with me."

This "think of it this way" eases traveling today. We pass a cemetery: I feel superior and sniff inwardly, "None of *my* concern!"

What you sow does not come to life unless it dies. When you sow, you do not plant the body that will be, but just a seed, perhaps of wheat or of something else. . . . So will it be with the resurrection of the dead. The body that is sown is perishable, it is raised imperishable; it is sown in dishonor, it is raised in glory; it is sown in weakness, it is raised in power; it is sown a natural body, it is raised a spiritual body.

1 Corinthians 15:36–37, 42–44

> And if the Spirit of him who raised Jesus from the dead is living in you, he who raised Christ from the dead will also give life to your mortal bodies through his Spirit, who lives in you.
>
> Romans 8:11

Saturday, July 13 We are settled into a housekeeping cabin in a small tourist town central to Cape Breton. The region's precipiced coasts and crescent harbors do deliver their promised magic—dazzling and relaxing and buoying our spirits. Viewed from mountain slopes, small skiffs painted in primary red, blue, yellow, orange, and green ride like enameled toys on the dark water of village coves. With binoculars we join others at elevated lookouts, spotting whales; we are mesmerized by the faraway, private play we glimpse tiny against the ocean.

Monday, July 15 Jack is off hiking to a waterfall, and I sit at the town's waterfront reading *Grief and Growth* by Scott Sullender. It is written for persons grieving the loss of another and also for persons approaching their own death. One chapter explores the apostle Paul's experience of afflictions, delineating their deepening of his life in the present and also their creating within him an intense longing for what is ahead—the experience of glory, of being united with Christ. The author describes grieving as a time of creativity and deepened spirituality.

As the sun heightens in the sky, I keep pursuing seating that includes shade. From a distance, I covet a lone tree banked with toys and gym bags near which several older teens are supervising half a dozen small children who are playing at the water's edge. The teens' conversation, just out of earshot, swims through and around their watchfulness of the children. They also settle altercations, lotion noses and limbs, and portion out snacks. Angle my book as I must, cower beneath the brim of my hat as I must, the easy nurture of the scene gives shade to my spirit as I read *Grief and Growth.*

I recall Jonah relishing the vine that grew up in a day, thus blessing him with shade, followed by his angry despair when it withered. And God's reminder to him that in a much greater way he, God, cherishes human beings. Yes, God is cherishing me right now. I feel his Spirit's gentleness: The glare-bright words, so helpful and apt to my situation, speak of his choosing this book for me, of his having guided my hand to select it earlier this morning.

The pages draw me forward into a prizing of grief, or at least into a utilization of its heightened awareness and intent faith. The author uses a word I've not heard often in the last decades (although I did in my childhood, when doctrinal language swirled its outline neatness onto sermons, school lessons, and adult talk): *sanctification.* A process. And I love process. Especially process that brings about greater and greater good, which so often happens for a person receiving psychotherapy, which remains one of my greatest earthly joys. These pages trace out Paul's process as he experienced afflictions. He simply became more and more focused on Christ, cherishing in his imagination the coming bliss of being in Christ's presence. His afflictions changed him into more and more of what he was supposed to be: a creature of God's fashioning who loved God above all else.

And we, who with unveiled faces all reflect the Lord's glory, are being transformed into his likeness with ever-increasing glory, which comes from the Lord, who is the Spirit.

2 Corinthians 3:18

So, Mirth, this agony of being torn away from loved ones can become a transforming process, a being-sculpted-into-beauty process for a believer. Don't think about the lungs being eaten away, the metastases (to the brain would be the worst), the months of wasting, the vulture pain, the tearful faces around the bed. Think about an increasing love for God, more longing for intimacy with him, more freedom from the fierce possessiveness you now have of those whom you love, a possessiveness that is breaking your heart. You are in the very best process you could be in—a transformation that starts now in time and gets completed in eternity. Square your shoulders and enter into it with determination. This is the best process that you will ever experience in this life.

Better than delivering a child? Better than shaping a marriage? Better than winning the trust of a battered client? Better than leading a person to Christ, into new freedom in his emotional life, into new freedom in her spiritual life?

Later I climb the three long, steep blocks back to the cabin. I have to rest more than once. What is so startling and sobering is the panting for breath.

Friday, July 19 Today we are in Wolfsville, a university town that has a theater for Shakespearean plays. Before the play we browse the boutiques. I'm really out of shape; can't keep up with Jack's strides. He shows me the design of a greeting card: It is black, with a white calla lily flower, its tall, teal-green stem and leaf regal against the dark. With a white inscription: "We cannot direct the wind, but we can adjust our sails." It blesses us. We buy it.

Tuesday, July 23 I brought along a pile of church papers for some catch-up reading during vacation. Today a headline in one of them caught my eye. It was about the New Jerusalem being the bride of Christ. A belfry-sized gong struck. So simple. So enormous. So unbelievable that I had missed it. When I see God face-to-face I will do so as part of an innumerable multitude, *all of whom* are entranced by his glory, *all of whom* are absorbing his beauty and perfection. It will take an innumerable multitude to absorb the glory of God! Whatever have I been thinking of! Unconsciously I have been assuming that he and I will be over against each other . . . tête-à-tête . . . whatever made me think that? I am baffled and embarrassed by my unconscious spiritual gaffe.

I figure it out. This comes from doing therapy. The therapist sits with the client with attentiveness that is both keen and relaxed, accepting and alert, as pleasurable as friendship and, when necessary, as incisive as a knife. Nothing is unimportant: The look away, the involuntary hand movement, the slight flush, the changed subject . . . all are clues to unconscious or unarticulated processes that clothe the client's dilemma. I am so accustomed to this professional hyper-awareness that I brought it to my assumptions about being in the presence of God. I expected to be held in an exquisite tension of focus, trembling like a harp to his beauty, breathing in rhythm to the throb of his glory . . . no wonder the hugeness of that encounter has been making me a little frantic, evoking the message from my core, "You are not ready . . . not ready . . ." I am just a puny little *creature*, I cannot handle the infinite . . . although with all my heart I trust him for salvation, for forgiveness, for eternal life. I have been really mixed up.

I now relax as I melt into the innumerable throng who see God, see the Son. It takes the innumerable to be apposite to the glory of God. Why did I without thinking take this on by myself? Was it simply because of the model I practice professionally? Was it arrogance, independence, a tendency to operate out of my own thoughts and strength? Was it just silliness, stupidity? Perhaps it is my push toward intimacy, toward the interior of a relationship. I know that fear had me in its grip. Perhaps it is an experience of grace, that already in this life I apprehend in the dimmest of ways Godness, Holiness, Otherness, I Am-ness . . . and know that he is so far beyond my capacity for response that all the believers who ever lived are together needed for that response.

And yet, God called Abraham his friend. And Jesus loved John in a special way. One on one. But God accommodated himself to them by giving them brief visions or the hearing of his voice, or incarnated himself into a human form. In eternity the partialness and veiling will be gone, and we will see him face-to-face. *With the throng* I will tremble to his beauty.

"After this I looked and there before me was a great multitude that no one could count, from every nation, tribe, people and language, standing before the throne and in front of the Lamb. They were wearing white robes and were holding palm branches in their hands. And they cried out in a loud voice: 'Salvation belongs to our God, who sits on the throne, and to the Lamb.' . . . Then one of the elders asked me, 'These in white robes—who are they, and where did they come from?' I answered, 'Sir, you know.' And he said, 'These are they who have come out of the great tribulation; they have washed their robes and made them white in the blood of the Lamb. Therefore, they are before the throne of God and serve him day and night in his temple; and he who sits on the throne will spread his tent over them'" (Rev. 7:9–10, 13–15).

Now we see but a poor reflection as in a mirror; then we shall see face to face. Now I know in part; then I shall know fully, even as I am fully known.

1 Corinthians 13:12

Blessed are the pure in heart, for they will see God.

Matthew 5:8

FRIDAY, JULY 26 A garden bursting with produce welcomed us home two days ago with an onslaught of beans needing immediate attention. Between client sessions I sit on the deck, snapping off ends, competing with myself by varying the numbers of beans in the handfuls I grab, experimenting to find the most efficient way. Thousands of rippled yellow-green shafts slip through my fingers in mindless rhythm, creating a subliminal song: *I am leaving this yard, I am leaving this garden, I am leaving this deck, I am leaving this cycle of seasons, I am leaving, I am leaving, I am leaving, I am leaving.* Thousands, perhaps millions, of times this soundless thinking of the unthinkable thinks itself into my brain, thinks and thinks, thinks and thinks. The dinning is strident and dull. I feel tenderness toward my poor brain, faithfully trying to retool itself.

Is this the last time I will prepare beans for the freezer? Later, making strawberry jam—the final time of hulling, crushing, boiling, stirring, pouring, sealing? The hovering question is asked by the narrow-eyed, rueful smile Jack and I exchange as he enters the kitchen.

TUESDAY, JULY 30 I wonder how many persons are renovating homes when the diagnosis of cancer that will not be cured drops into their lives? The experience must be fairly common . . . but the juxtapositioning of the two in my life right now is very *odd.* For many months glossy pictures of plans for various rooms in this house have collaged gallery walls inside my head; now these plans are scrunched in a corner, pale papers kicked at idly by my mind. We were building for an extended future: These were the rooms in which we would be l . . i . . v . . i . . n . . g . . . a . . . l . . o . . n . . g . . . t . . i . . m . . e. Without my living in them, what is the point? Without me, why would Jack live in this house at all, a large house with an office area? *There is no longer any point.*

It seems that God is mocking the pleasure we had, pleasure in searching out tiles and cabinets and wallpaper. It seems that God is mocking our blind presumption.

Today a tradesman is laying ceramic tile in the bathroom. Its perfect color, its perfect design is steadily blocking over the dirty beige-brown of the old floor.

The emerging beauty soothes my stupidity. I realize that God is not mocking us. He's interrupting us, certainly, and the reason is that transcendent activity of his own, which our transient efforts palely imitate: the designing, constructing, preparing, and making beautiful of a living space, a house. The telling of it is so familiar: "Do not let your hearts be troubled. Trust in God, trust also in me. In my Father's house are many rooms; if it were not so, I would have told you. I am going there to prepare a place for you. And if I go and prepare a place for you, I will come back and take you to be with me that you also may be where I am. You know the way to the place where I am going" (John 14:1–4).

A stretch? Marbled green ceramic tile linked with being taken to live with Jesus? Perhaps. But God is not mocking what we are doing. He is doing his own God-work, and he smiles on us as we flex in his image, making beautiful rooms.

The wall was made of jasper, and the city of pure gold, as pure as glass. The foundations of the city walls were decorated with every kind of precious stone. The first foundation was jasper, the second sapphire, the third chalcedony, the fourth emerald, the fifth sardonyx, the sixth carnelian, the seventh chrysolite, the eighth beryl, the ninth topaz, the tenth chrysoprase, the eleventh jacinth, and the twelfth amethyst. The twelve gates were twelve pearls, each gate made of a single pearl. The great street of the city was of pure gold, like transparent glass.

Revelation 21:18–21

TUESDAY, AUGUST 6 The first half of today I resisted sitting at the computer, resisted going on with these lava gouts of grief. But I must continue "to let words work the earth of my heart" as Kathleen Norris writes in *The Cloister Walk*.

I am reading C. S. Lewis's *A Grief Observed*. It's a special gift he has left for all believers who mourn—the sharing of his bitter wrestle with God following the death of his wife after a brief, intensely happy marriage. His bewilderment pushes him to dare try on the concept of God as a cold vivisectionist rather than a loving healer. And this is the same man who had shaped biblical details about eternal life into fantastic, lucidly compelling stories that evoke a "Yes!" from readers, a "Yes!" that includes stirrings of joy! His grief is as harrowing as anyone else's.

This comforts me. There is no escape. Believing, comprehending at depth, being gifted by God with genius for discerning biblical truth, do not save a person from the rack. It's that attachment problem: the tearing.

Deeply poignant is his describing that in the early stages of grief he cannot conjure up his wife's face, though he is desperate to remember it. Later his life plods forward into new routines without her; and then, paradoxically, memory brings her vividly to him.

I seem to be searching out pilgrims on the grief path who have left some guideposts for us who follow. In the church library I recently found *A Severe Mercy,* written by C. S. Lewis's friend Sheldon Van Auken about the death of his own wife. He describes what he calls "the second death," when the bereaved person has exhausted his or her mourning and the loved person is no longer an omnipresent memory. Initially, the agony of grieving maintains a kind of involvement with the loved person, but when the grieving process is completed after several years, true aloneness sets in.

So Jack will walk sorrow's walk. And, in less intense ways, my children. At times they will be called to its path again, stricken by new deaths, walking the road of grieving and recovering . . . until each one reaches his and her own death. Why then do I experience the beckoning of *mine* as such a scandalous affront! I'm ashamed and baffled by my persistent sadness, my rebellion, my feeling sometimes of being trapped.

But perhaps what seems like self-centered ego is really a remnant of Paradise, when humans were created with eternity in their hearts. The yells inside that I cannot suppress are inverted hymns to the beauty of God's original design. The more I hurt, the more I bear witness to what once was. To what was ruined.

He has made everything beautiful in its time. He has also set eternity in the hearts of men

Ecclesiastes 3:11

> *All men are like grass, and all their glory is like the flowers of the field. The grass withers and the flowers fall, because the breath of the LORD blows on them. Surely the people are grass. The grass withers and the flowers fall, but the word of our God stands forever.*
>
> Isaiah 40:6–8

Then I remember the dazzle of eternal life. There—just beyond death's gauntlet arch.

SUNDAY, AUGUST 18 Many visits. We host an overnight stay of five relatives. A four-day visit of a friend who is single after many years of marriage. Several afternoon visits of out-of-town friends and of former clients.

It is getting increasingly hard to fudge these situations and enact bright normalcy. It is harder on Jack than myself. His attentiveness greys out now and then. Yet we have agreed that we will tell everybody about my illness at the same time, because it will be hard for persons to bear it individually, which will cause each to tell at least one other person, who will do likewise, and then the fact of it will run like outgoing tide through the communities in which we have lived, to leap back via friendships into our present community before we can share it here ourselves. I'm not accustomed to hypocrisy, to leaning on the kitchen counter trying to get enough breath, then sallying forth to serve cold drinks and cookies. Do I appear drawn, I wonder, as at one level my weariness ticks off the minutes of the encounters, while at another I am savoring the presence of these people whom I love? And how angry they will be that we did not tell them! That is frightening.

Tuesday, August 20 Denial works for each of us when we want it to badly enough. I told Jack he need not come with me to the oncologist appointment today because I think I have been doing quite well. Mysteriously, the pain has been absent this last week. He mentions my coughing in my sleep, which he listens to in the night, and my occasional deep gasp for breath. But I am optimistic and go alone.

She is terse today. "The Tamoxifen is not working." It is almost an accusation. "There is a new site of cancer—the lower right lung." She shows me the X ray. To my naive eye the whitish spread in that area is enormous, hardly believable, bewildering. Its edges resemble those of a sprawling spiderweb. "We need to start the chemo right away. It will not prolong your life, but it will maintain the quality of your life."

I am truly in shock. The requisite scenario spirals itself out: I must share my plight with others now, since I will be losing my hair; I will need to assist my clients through the termination of therapy with me (I remember the intense concern of clients that had to be faced six years ago); I must make the most of my time with my family; and I must prepare to receive scrutiny from hundreds of people with whom I have shared significant experiences. And keep on preparing to die. The bit of control that we had is gone; that creepy, creeping whiteness is now in control.

Thursday, August 22 How have I been so blind? I have to rest on the landing to catch my breath when I come upstairs from my office. I cough and clear my throat often. I'm too tired to carry in groceries. After five minutes on the NordicTrack™ I'm ready to stop. And I've been telling myself I'm just out of shape? Today, after seeing five clients, I cried from weariness.

I got tucked into bed.

SUNDAY, AUGUST 25 We drive to church in "time standing still" quietness. What we feel is not exactly dread but deep regret. In the hall before the service, a woman asks how I am. The pleasantry cuts; because we have gotten to know one another "at depth," I have to prepare her: I blurt, "Actually, not too well. The cancer I had some years ago has returned. Jack will make an announcement about it this morning." The swirl of parishioners separates me from her startled face. But it helps me that I have told her. During the service I take comfort in knowing that another person is waiting, braced like myself.

The sermon is about the resurrection. Jack's delivery is passionate. Other ears would not pick up that his voice is pitched imperceptibly higher than usual, but I notice the increment of strain. When he ends, the congregation murmurs "Amen." The offering is taken. Together the congregation enters the pause in which prayer needs are shared. In a strained voice, breaking once, Jack reads the announcement about my illness, its terminal prognosis, the treatment already begun, the ending of my practice by October. He proceeds to the intercessory prayer. Behind me a friend cries softly. Likewise the woman in front of me, and the woman in front of her. "Good!" I think savagely. It is only right. I put my hand on the shoulder of the woman ahead and she lifts her hand to mine, a clasping we keep until the prayer ends. My own tears silent on my cheeks.

The afterward is exactly as we had visualized it: persons lining up to hug us, then holding us, saying how sorry they are, wiping tears from their eyes. I do not know where Jack is nor he, me, because of the crowding. These sympathizing people do not have long-term relationships with us; we have lived here for only two years; perhaps a handful knew my cancer history. Yet, because we are believers, we are a family. And while this is happening here, our news is also being shared in two former congregations Jack has served.

The "family" that cares about us today consists of hundreds. Each person will pick up a piece of our grief and help us carry it.

My boundaries dissolve. I feel that I am leaking out into the amorphous cloud of kindness and sadness that engulfs the room.

It is time to go home.

The body is a unit, though it is made up of many parts; and though all its parts are many, they form one body. . . . If one part suffers, every part suffers with it.

1 Corinthians 12:12, 26

. . . so in Christ we who are many form one body, and each member belongs to all the others.

Romans 12:5

Rejoice with those who rejoice; mourn with those who mourn.

Romans 12:15

Tuesday, August 27 This chemo clinic is quite a bit like the one in the city in which I lived in 1990. Then I was intrigued by its system, curious about the nurses, touched by their care. But today I feel surly and ungrateful. I am given pamphlets about my drugs, shown a video about possible reactions to them, gifted with a stocked toiletries bag from the drugstore conglomerate that is swallowing up all its competitors. I turn away from the posters of smiling women wearing turbans. Who is kidding whom? Whom have you ever seen wearing a turban, anyway? I hate these trappings—the sappy helpful materials, the cheery nurses, the poison bags on wheeled white rigs. In this long room filled with haggard persons in La-Z-Boy chairs, *I* see a hooded, brightly flowered, terry robe sashaying about, concealing in its folds—death.

September

WEDNESDAY, SEPTEMBER 4 Today several clients and I faced my illness and its ending our therapeutic work. The clients abused as children are especially stricken. "God always takes away something good that I have." "This is a sign that I am not supposed to be in therapy, not supposed to get better." "I can't imagine starting over with a new therapist. I'll just stop now with what I've gained so far." "God has deceived me."

I knew these reactions were coming. They are what I have dreaded, the reason I have kept my illness from them for four months. Because my task is healing, with every fiber of my being I want to make these persons' lives better, not give them more pain.

Yet their egocentric responses are signs of new stages of emotional health. These persons, violated and humiliated in their formative years, trust their relationship with me in a way that they have never trusted anyone as children.

Their transparent responses resemble those of children aged six or eight or ten who do not have to be guarded with parents, because they have been allowed to blurt out difficult thoughts and feelings, which are then taken seriously. Children given the building blocks of self-worth: attentiveness and respect. My clients. Respected by me. More and more respecting themselves.

I ache for them. In my experience, abused persons who are Christian believers require a longer time to recover from their trauma than persons of other faiths or persons who have no religious faith. It is so terribly hard to reconcile bad things with a belief in God who is himself Love! (I should know; I'm withdrawing from professional work to have the energy to sort out my own grief and rebellion.)

We flounder in the sessions, noting how one's experience of parents unconsciously shapes one's experience of God—as withholding, perhaps, or stupid, cold, disinterested, favoring others, arbitrary. With the addition, for some, of overt abuse: "God never protected me from the beatings, the fondling, the forced acts, although I begged him to, praying over and over, believing my Sunday school teacher when she said that God was my friend and would always help me."

As a former client told me, "My family never went to church, but when I was young I would put on my little sweater and bike to the service, hoping that God would see me there and rescue me."

Therefore pride is their necklace; they clothe themselves with violence. From their callous hearts comes iniquity; the evil conceits of their minds know no limits. They scoff, and speak with malice; in their arrogance they threaten oppression. Their mouths lay claim to heaven, and their tongues take possession of the earth. They say, "How can God know? Does the Most High have knowledge?"

Psalm 73:6–9, 11

God and the fact of evil. God who creates the structure of the family, giving to parents the task of mediating unconditional love to a child. God who does not intervene when they don't. God who does not use lightning bolts to zap the abuser—or to kill the cancer that eats tissue. God who disrupts important relationships. The God who disappoints.

With my clients I can only share what I am personally doing with my grief: struggling it out with God, trying to live each day within the entirety of biblical revelation, so that my faith-sight gets unspectacled from the dark lenses of experience with humans and cleared of the projections I've smeared onto God. I share how Philip Yancey's book *Disappointment with God* has been helping me since 1986 when I first read it, and how I learned from it that the Bible is not a record of God making people's lives work but a record of God's seeking a relationship of love with the humans he created. And his acting in Christ to bring that about, in earthly life imperfectly, in eternity, in perfection.

Clients ask, "What's the use then of having a God? I want a God who is powerful, who protects me and makes things better."

Before these persons feel love for a God who does not do magic for them, there are more lengths of emotional healing they must traverse. I reassure them that God is holding on to them, even while their response to him is numbed. This is what I trust for myself, too, as I question and fight the prospect of my death. But much of my clients' quarrel with God is at bottom a quarrel with people. With people who, in *their* turn, have been poorly served by *other* people. My clients' quarrel is with sin. And my quarrel is with sin's crudest form, death.

The Spirit is present as we, the disappointed ones, talk with each other in the counseling room. He intercedes for us. Lord, we believe. Help our unbelief.

I remember that God's quarrel, too, is with sin and death.

Immediately the boy's father exclaimed, "I do believe; help me overcome my unbelief!"

Mark 9:24

. . . but because Jesus lives forever, he has a permanent priesthood. Therefore he is able to save completely those who come to God through him, because he always lives to intercede for them.

Hebrews 7:24–25

In the same way, the Spirit helps us in our weakness. We do not know what we ought to pray for, but the Spirit himself intercedes for us with groans that words cannot express. And he who searches our hearts knows the mind of the Spirit, because the Spirit intercedes for the saints in accordance with God's will.

Romans 8:26–27

"And I pray that you, being rooted and established in love, may have power, together with all the saints, to grasp how wide and long and high and deep is the love of Christ, and to know this love that surpasses knowledge—that you may be filled to the measure of all the fullness of God" (Ephesians 3:17–19).

Thursday, September 5 It is happening now, the inrush of concern from the many people who have been part of our lives through thirty-five years of pastoral ministry and thirteen years of psychotherapy practice. It enters through the openings of our home: The mailbox spills over, white florists' boxes get carried in, dear people phone, many of them from the past. I talked with a woman today with whom I had not spoken for twenty-five years. Yesterday I received a group card from women who were with me in a Bible study during that same period. Decades collapse into immediacy, the faces of these persons rising up before me as substantial as the kitchen table.

Friday, September 6 The texture of these days is atypical. Love wraiths our home like fragrance, haloes our heads, breathes upon our bodies. I discover myself trembling emotionally; I feel shy. So many fervent, warm voices and letters—so many steadfast, earnest assurances of continual prayer for Jack and myself—I cry out to God for adequacy of spirit.

But I know what is happening, something exactly right. (And how rare in life, how stock-still-strikingly awesome, to receive what is exactly right!) I've shared with many persons a dance of faith renewal, or of emotional healing, or of spiritual or intellectual exchange; and now each person is catching me up in further measures, newly patterned by my extremity. What is overwhelming me is an enormous cotillion of friendship and intimacy: I may not draw back from it but instead must dip my body to its swath, engaging turn upon turn with those who offer me new steps.

For when we came into Macedonia, this body of ours had no rest, but we were harassed at every turn—conflicts on the outside, fears within. But God, who comforts the downcast, comforted us by the coming of Titus, and not only by his coming but also by the comfort you had given him. He told us about your longing for me, your deep sorrow, your ardent concern for me, so that my joy was greater than ever.

2 Corinthians 7:5–7

WEDNESDAY, SEPTEMBER 11 The letters I am receiving run the gamut from reminiscences to farewells to celebrations to stubborn reiterations that I must live and that the writer(s) will keep on "storming heaven's gate" for my recovery. This startles me! This approach lifts into awareness my trusting acceptance of medical pronouncements, turning it over as a ladle would, pouring it out, finding it wanting. Grieving acceptance is just not sufficiently *robust,* I now realize. I am so cheered by others telling me that they pray for a miracle!

More, I'm mesmerized and dazzled. This beseeching of God to heal me that my friends write about—may I practice this myself? Has my spirit been waiting for others to show me how to do this? Is God teaching me right now that such praying can fit together with my taking his hand and walking forward toward eternal life? My friends are pouring over me the joy of asking, the faith of asking, the persistence of asking. I revel in it, like a child dancing in a sprinkler on a hot day.

> You prepare a table before me in the presence of my enemies. You anoint my head with oil; my cup overflows.
>
> Psalm 23:5

> In the course of my life he broke my strength; he cut short my days. So I said, "Do not take me away, O my God, in the midst of my days . . ."
>
> Psalm 102:23–24

THURSDAY, SEPTEMBER 19 This afternoon a silent shriek ripped inside my head. I read four lengthy letters in succession, each beautifully and thoughtfully written, detailing good things about our interactions, each taking the form of a kind of salute. Bitterness flash-fired my gut—"Oh, I may be so wonderful and everything, but *I* still have to *die!*"

That is what I am learning about this grief thing. There's so much anger at its core. People love me and tell me why, and I turn my head, experiencing their kindness as the hearing of eulogies at my own funeral. They celebrate who I am, and I have the eerie feeling that I am being rolled up like a rug to be laid away on a shelf. If they say nothing about my predicament, I'm indignant (not expressed, of course) and feel all awry. I am not to be pleased; my responses are irrational, I hate this focus on myself, I cry from the hyper-emotionality of it all. Grief is a mixed-up mess, and I am not a nice person in my grief.

MONDAY, SEPTEMBER 23 Like others' prayers for me, something else seems to be soaking hopefulness into my dryness. Many persons are sharing with me the information they have about alternative therapies. Apologizing for intruding but pushed forward by concern, they offer books, videos, photocopied sheets, brochures, telephone numbers of homeopathic and naturopathic practitioners, addresses of clinics in Nevada and Mexico. Their diffidence touches my heart, because it shows they've known rebuff. But not from me; I'm very grateful, softly comforted by the fact of their attention. Some of these people I hardly know.

I remember the Cancer Society's book. Why is this experience so different? I need faces, I guess. The faces, the eyes, give weight to the remedies, separating out some from the many.

WEDNESDAY, SEPTEMBER 25 Today we visited a chiropractor in a nearby town. The trail to her office began when a family member recently was immobilized by a back problem, was taken by ambulance to the hospital, was told by the ambulance attendants about this practitioner, received an appointment, told her about me in the process of being treated himself—and found out she had a patient who had *had* lung cancer but now had only one benign node left on her lung (!!!).

So events link into a chain of inevitability. I have adopted a new regimen. After the chiropractor described the effectiveness of various powdered nutrients, which taken together are believed to boost the immune system's ability to fight cancer cells, I had no hesitation. (Jack was a little wary, hearing her aver that a person's not living out a biblical "three score years and ten" was contrary to God's will for that person.) She suggested that we become distributors of the products to somewhat reduce their cost. She handed me a dosage chart.

This stuff. Vitality verily leaps from the opened jars. Powdered barley and kelp, garbage bag green. Powdered organic carrots, neon orange. Powdered beets, blazing fuchsia. Powdered protein, chalky cream. Powdered fiber and minerals, grit grey. The first three shaken together in water to algaed-swamp-water consistency and imbibed forty minutes before a meal. The last two shaken together in water into granular sludge and imbibed twenty minutes before a meal. The aftermath to each a gagging shudder. These are power drinks, for sure!

But it feels great to be *doing* something. I'm a little hyper with the new hope. I praise God for the ambulance attendants, my family member's sharing my plight—even for the back problem (which has not been solved).

Thursday, September 26 Since certain substances get recurring mention in various printouts, the remedies have sorted themselves out into a list I decide to ingest. Essiac tea. Shark cartilage. Silenium. Bio-Pectin. As well as all the vitamins I've been taking for years. Plus free-range meat and eggs, if one can't become a vegetarian outright. Low fat and no sugar. No processed foods. Fiber to the max, as well as vegetables and fruits.

Some of these food protocols I've followed for years. Yet cancer recurred. As to all the rest, isn't it a bit like locking the barn after the horse has been stolen?

When I tell my oncologist my routine, she is noncommittal, or perhaps mildly affirming. She mentions that taking any action is beneficial in that it gives the patient a sense of control.

Yes.

SATURDAY, SEPTEMBER 28 A sibling and her spouse make a long trek to visit us. She says, "When you die, part of me will die, too, because you remember the way it was."

October

TUESDAY, OCTOBER 1 X ray result day, after three chemotherapy treatments, each a month apart. Emotionally flat and fearful, we sit in the waiting room, the familiar precipice edge sharp under our feet. As we are ushered into the oncologist's narrow examining room, Jack says softly to me, "The Lord's strength will carry us through." Together we almost fill the small galley, he standing against the wall, I sitting on the examining table.

"Come look at the X ray!" She is at the door, her beautiful face open and animated. On a wall of her jumbled office the August and the October X rays are posted side by side. The whitish spread at the bottom of the left lung is much smaller in the October picture. I see the words "significantly shrunk" written on a manila envelope. We are stunned. She beams.

Jack asks whether just the inflammation has subsided, but she assures us that the cancer itself has been reduced. I ask whether this is usual—I want to hear that it is not and that it must be my diet that is accomplishing this—and she replies yes, it is usual; this is what the chemotherapy is supposed to do.

I realize that it is the poison, not the nutrition, that is her tool and that she is exhilarated when it works.

We had not hoped for this much, only that the cancer had not spread further. We walk to the elevator in a soft daze. No matter that my white blood count was too low for me to have the chemo treatment today. Something is working. The horizon lengthens. . . . Hey, it SHRUNK!

WEDNESDAY, OCTOBER 2 I have a second terribly fast growing entity within me. Hope.

Cheerfully I adjust to the demands of this day, not nauseous as I had expected to be, since the chemo has been postponed. Hope is sprawling its tentacles through my limbs and brain, giving me brisk movements, squeezing the brain cells to emit a cheerful sotto voce aria that goes like this: "Oh, it's great; God is going to glorify himself by doing a miracle in me . . . I'll take this year to be sick, I'll write, and then I'll begin my practice again . . . and believers everywhere will tell with joy what God has done for me . . . I'll share with others my health regimen . . . Jack and I will be so happy, we will radiate praise to God . . ." I am nine-tenths oblivious to the merry obbligato, just serenely go through the day, at peace.

In the evening there is time to take up the book *Quantum Healing* by Deepak Chopra. I read attentively, waiting for the punch-line idea toward which the chapters must be building. Then I am reading the sentence on page 92: "If a patient comes to me with lung cancer, even early detection is no help. I can give him radiation and call it a therapy, but in 95 percent of the cases it is little more than a short reprieve—perhaps he and I go through it just to fend off the despair of having no treatment at all." I suddenly *hear* the merry song, just as it crashes into discord, heavy songbook falling on the keys.

That messy hope has got me again. Pain's teeth tearing me, again.

What is worse: low-grade grief sobering each day and ending with weak tears each night—or calm days and tearless nights slashed now and again by death's inexorable fact, tumbling me about in a torment of grief, fierce as that of the first knowing?

Do I have a choice? I am just a human. Facing death, my emotions careen every which way, sometimes designing illusions of safety, sometimes painting heartbreaking scenes of suffering and farewell. Sometimes, if I steep myself in his Word, valuing the immediacy of being fully in fellowship with God.

I accept my humanness; I will keep on careening. After all, Jesus wrapped humanness about himself, honoring it, walking around in it, shuddering too as he looked toward his own terrible end. I wonder if he ever forgot for an hour or two what was coming—if he ever thought his Father might design another way—or sometimes gasped, feeling panic that he was getting closer with each passing month?

No panic, I realize. I think that unlike me he was able to keep it all together all the time. Dread, perhaps, but no careening. He *wanted* to do it so that human creatures, I, clinging to the familiarity of earthly life with almost perverse attachment, might have safe passage into *real* life. He felt the fear and he still wanted to do it.

As the time approached for him to be taken up to heaven, Jesus resolutely set out for Jerusalem.

Luke 9:51

The reason my Father loves me is that I lay down my life—only to take it up again. No one takes it from me, but I lay it down of my own accord. I have authority to lay it down and authority to take it up again. This command I received from my Father.

John 10:17–18

For we do not have a high priest who is unable to sympathize with our weaknesses, but we have one who has been tempted in every way, just as we are—yet was without sin. Let us then approach the throne of grace with confidence, so that we may receive mercy and find grace to help us in our time of need.

Hebrews 4:15–16

I feel his Spirit helping me out of the boat again and locking my gaze into his. I walk toward him. The water is cold but buoyant under my feet.

Wednesday, October 9 Many people call to set up a visit. Jack and I get out our appointment books, looking for slots not filled by other business, slots to be matched with a list of names. We leaf forward into the November weeks.

Gush of tears. These ruled pages shorthand the passage of time to a deeper level of consciousness than the level that matches names and slots. I cannot bear this sequence of paged weeks and months; their turning shows time running out. The "Live one day at a time, and make it a masterpiece"—that is the only timeline I can handle. I have disconnected the synapses that create predictions and possibilities. I have been contenting myself that the rest of my life is to be a surprise, teaching myself to stop anticipating *anything*. The date book shatters the ploy.

> *Who of you by worrying can add a single hour to his life?*
>
> *Matthew 6:27*

FRIDAY, OCTOBER 11 Serendipity. Synchronicity. Providence. I can take my pick. Astonishingly, I have in my possession certain objects that now move front and forward to address my illness with bold eloquence. The *picture* I've had for fifteen years. The *rock*, four. The *compact disc*, three. They've been in my home and office, enjoyed, loved—but now they engage my grief as if all the previous having of them has been surface pleasure. Does a God who is upholding the universe bother with details like this—putting objects into my life so that they will be there for this time of slash and ache? My eyes widen with astonishment, my head shakes *no*, half disbelief, half wonder.

But. The disc. Bought when Jack and I attended a male chorus concert and found the program to be shared by a contemporary Christian rock group. (We know little about either type of music; we were there unexpectedly.) The two final songs on the group's disc are "The Race of Time" and "The New Jerusalem." If I play the preceding two tracks as well, I get twenty minutes of music, the perfect amount for my NordicTrack™ exercise routine. The beat is insistent; by increments it pushes my body forward into that lovely space of effortless moving, ever faster, pleasurably panting. The language is biblical: "You've run the race of time./ You've reached the goal I've set/ and now, my child, it's time I brought you home." And later, ". . . the city is more beautiful than we have ever known,/ for the love of God is brighter than the sun." What a high! Every other day. I can't play anything else anymore; I just keep running the race and joining in the "Holy, Holy, Holy" at the end, dropping the machine's reins, lifting my arms, crying sometimes.

Did you make sure I would have these songs, God?

The picture. Across the room. It's four photographs, actually, matted in black, mounted side by side in one silver-colored frame. The photographs consist of black smudges that together create the Gestalt of a woman: She has been photographed through a screen so that the camera has picked up only indistinct splotches of body. The figure is in motion, first bent over at the waist, then rising a bit, and then more fully, until the last picture shows her upright, limbs flung wide, free.

My artist friend allowed me to select these four prints from a larger work she had made of twenty-four such photographs. I wanted them fifteen years ago because the evolving freedom in them portrayed to me the process of psychotherapy. The large work created by the four had pride of place in my new office. Although I had not intended it to be so, it became a kind of Rorschach image for many clients, usually an unpleasant one. One of my partners referred to it as "your picture of that person trapped in a shower stall." But the designer who installed the office blinds said, "I love your dancers!" So projection.

Now it hangs in my family room cum waiting room cum exercise room, and the woman is taken up into the songs, into the race, into reaching Jerusalem. The fresh projection: She depicts my life, its turn and swirl, its bracing against, its vigorous and searching movements. And that fourth picture, final liberation. Looking at it often, moving in rhythm, I drench myself in realities that can, that *must* dilute my grief, can and *must* wash me in certainty that what's ahead is going to be so much . . . greater? better? whatever? . . . than the now. I've lived with these smudges for so long . . . and now they beckon me . . . on.

The rock. (It's not in this room but in my desk drawer, with devotional stuff.) It's fat and stubby, with a flat bottom, about three and a half inches high. Painted on it is the face of Jesus—yes!, the familiar handsome bearded face of Caucasian myth. The artist? A Buddhist nun convert to Christianity who lives in a tiny boat house on the shore of Lake Ontario, who takes as canvas stones cast up by the water's roil. She finds in their strata the outline of a cheek or beard, the rise of a shoulder, the drape of a robe. Larger rocks suggest to her entire Gospel scenes, their contours yielding up crowds and landscape. Most of her portraits of Christ are on flat stones; so mine, her parting gift when we moved away, is unusual, in form more like a paperweight.

I've never had a picture of Jesus anywhere in any place I've ever lived. Reformation Protestant that I am, my conditioning leads me to keep distance from any human rendering of the divine. Cynicism toward sentimental Bible story book pictures is de rigueur for my crowd. But now this rock. It is useful to me. *It is useful to me.*

Jesus' face is turned to one side, his eyes downcast, his head bent. He is bearing a stilled form of suffering, with strength and patience. It may be his suffering at knowing men's hearts. It may be his suffering at having to hang out with the disciples, always so self-focused, always so selective in their listening. It may be his suffering rejection by those who knew Old Testament prophecy by heart. "Then everyone deserted him and fled" (Mark 14:50). It may be anticipatory suffering, dread of his being forsaken by God. "And at the ninth hour Jesus cried out in a loud voice, 'Eloi, eloi, lama sabachthani?'—which means, 'My God, my God, why have you forsaken me?'" (Mark 15:34).

If I were well, I would distance myself from this portrait on rock, while acknowledging the skill and love for Jesus that created it. But, distraught, I set it out to be with me as I seek God in private worship. Whatever I grieve moderates to the bearable when I gaze on his suffering. My situation is one of disappointment, fear, and mourning, but what Christ is bearing is different altogether—it's *suffering*. Contrariwise to what he experienced, I spend my life with persons who listen to me and understand me. I am not able to see the writhe of evil that chokes out good in a human heart. I will never be forsaken by God.

So I am humbled and led into praise-giving by this small rock.

Serendipity? Synchronicity? Providence? Objects I've had for years, become teachers and comforters? I pick *providence*.

> *Many, O LORD my God, are the wonders you have done. The things you planned for us no one can recount to you; were I to speak and tell of them, they would be too many to declare.*
>
> Psalm 40:5

MONDAY, OCTOBER 14 Canadian Thanksgiving Day. After cooking, table setting, and strategizing for an entire Saturday and Sunday about the traffic flow of my family in modest-sized rooms during a festive dinner and social time, I sit in the Thanksgiving Day worship service as engaged in the "now" as I possibly could be. Normalcy again—incurable illness at the farthest edges of notice—it is almost as if I am separated from it by a membrane that holds me like a fetus is held in its sac. As the image forms, I like it. That's what I am, a developing human getting ready to be birthed into eternity. I'm swaddled all around by stuff into which I invest energy and affection; I float and swoop around in it—unable to grasp that this fluid is ultimately constricting my existence. I grieve bitterly, in fact, whenever circumstances suggest this to me.

The image soothes me. I look around and see my fellow-worshippers in their sacs of this-life fluid. Perhaps I am the only one here who sees, because of the cancer. The star-child in the final frames of the movie *2001* flashes into my mind. If each of us worshipping here has the faith of a little child, we are all star-children of the Father. I will be fifty-nine tomorrow, and I am still a fetus in a sac.

> *Now we know that if the earthly tent we live in is destroyed, we have a building from God, an eternal house in heaven, not built by human hands. Meanwhile we groan, longing to be clothed with our heavenly dwelling, because when we are clothed, we will not be found naked. For while we are in this tent, we groan and are burdened, because we do not wish to be unclothed but to be clothed with our heavenly dwelling, so that what is mortal may be swallowed up by life. Now it is God who has made us for this very purpose and has given us the Spirit as a deposit, guaranteeing what is to come.*
>
> 2 Corinthians 5:1–5

For a few moments I hold the small view and the cosmic one in my mind at the same time. And it is very good.

Tuesday, October 15 Treatment day. Twelve of us sit in the oversized La-Z-Boy chairs that have adjustable armrests for our arms and hands, hands to which shunts are taped that connect with plastic vines hung on poles dangling bags of fluid.

A nice volunteer tells us that food is available. Some of the trussed ones order coffee and specify white bread sandwiches. I ask for herbal tea; they have none. Nutrition is not a concern here. This room's attendants, its patients, trust the poison.

My sidelong glance registers the woman next to me: good profile, hairless head sporting a baseball cap at a slight angle, long silver earrings of intricate design that the volunteers and nurses admire. Feeling a chill, she shrugs into a black suede jacket with a long-fringed yoke, stretching out tights-clad legs, handsome cowboy boots. The nurses and the volunteers hover; she is the quintessential cancer patient of newspaper stories—sassy, brave, chin tilted against the odds. The rest of us wait blankly, bodies lumped into sweats or pull-on pants.

The attendants talk of yesterday's Canadian Thanksgiving Day festivities . . . the turnip casserole, the pumpkin cheesecake. Their outfits are colored magenta or turquoise, or they wear smocks or jackets printed with magenta and turquoise blotches. Do they all buy these items from the same supplier? Is this supposed to be an improvement on white?

The double gravol dripping into my system dulls my low-grade rage. Then the poison dripping for an hour. A "flush" to finish off.

Home and many hours of sleep later, I wake to the chemicals' familiar attack on the brain's nausea center. They win at 3 A.M.: hot curdled stream . . . flush . . . brown burning spew . . . flush . . . stream spew phlegm . . . flush . . . heave . . . heave . . . flush.

Heave . . . yawn. I rest my forehead on the cool toilet rim and think of the day's headlines, the refugees in Zaire, without food or water, dying. And the little children . . .

it's beyond thinking about. Abba, Father, why am I one of the rich of the earth?

I thank him for the carpet beneath my knees, for the tissue, for the poison, for the research behind it, for Canada's health care that envelops me. For my bed.

For Jack's hand . . . whose fingertips now move over my face . . . a hypnotic touch that stills my whole body into slower breathing that will bring sleep. I sense the wedding ring on his moving hand and see its inscription inside: "Place me like a seal over your heart." Memory supplies the rest: "Place me like a seal over your heart, like a seal on your arm; for love is as strong as death, its jealousy unyielding as the grave. It burns like blazing fire, like a mighty flame. Many waters cannot quench love; rivers cannot wash it away. If one were to give all the wealth of his house for love, it would be utterly scorned" (Song of Songs 8:6–7).

Love and death. We are dealing with the verities, all right.

November

Saturday, November 9 At the cell leaders' breakfast meeting this week one of the leaders told a story that helps me. A rich man really wants to take something with him to heaven and does in fact get a special dispensation to do so. He arrives at heaven's gate and explains his special privilege to St. Peter, who asks to see what he has brought along. The man unwraps the ingot of gold he carries. St. Peter is nonplussed. "Paving!?" he says with astonishment.

I imagine the dispensation I want: that Jack and I will have our marriage in the richness of its present form forever into eternity. I receive my desire and explain it to St. Peter, who asks in astonishment, "Toddlerhood!? Forever!?"

Dear friends, now we are children of God, and what we will be has not yet been made known. But we know that when he appears, we shall be like him; for we shall see him as he is.

1 John 3:2

Now if we are children, then we are heirs—heirs of God and co-heirs with Christ, if indeed we share in his sufferings in order that we may also share in his glory. I consider that our present sufferings are not worth comparing with the glory that will be revealed in us.

Romans 8:17–18

Wednesday, November 13 A sleepless night. My thoughts in a cage, scrabbling at the bars. Better to get up in a house now cold because of the automatic lowering of the thermostat, wrap myself up in an afghan, and read. A friend has reminded me of the pungency of C. S. Lewis's *The Last Battle,* such an easy read I found this afternoon, when I got half-way.

I have read it before, of course, read all the Narnia stories, to each of my children in turn. And over the years I've sometimes reread the worn paperbacks on vacations. Tonight I hold a deluxe hardcover; Jack took delight in buying an expensive set a few years ago. Tonight the book in my hands is elegant; tonight I am reading to the frightened child in me.

Quite quickly I am stirred into wonder. First by the ending of the universe; then by the characters' induction into the dazzling, ever expanding heaven and earth. I say to Jack next morning, "It is *better* than the Book of Revelation," saying it somewhat hesitantly, feeling it to be a daring, irreverent statement, but at the same time feeling cupped in the hand of God. That is what the chapters have done, cupped me within God's enormous hand. But not only me; *you* are there, and *you*, and *you*, and *you*. That is what *this* story has: comradery, conversation, playfulness, excitement, limitless physical energy, a going forward and upward, vistas familiar but now radiating a piercing beauty . . . dazzle, fun, glory beyond compare. The cry is "further up" and "further in," and reality opens up, larger and larger, endlessly larger. With Aslan's tawny, enormous presence leaping joyously beside and among us, urging us on.

Typing this, I decide these chapters of *The Last Battle* bring the reader *up to* the finale of Revelation's last chapters. Like the afghan in my cold living room, Lewis's vision snuggles my fear of the unknown into warmth and *cheerfulness.* Amazing. For the first time *cheerfulness* about my death process enfolds me. I have to receive the Kingdom like a little child, and God gave his child Clive Staples a vision that my "child" can see. "Further up and further in." With everyone I love!

All the stars of the heavens will be dissolved and the sky rolled up like a scroll; all the starry host will fall like withered leaves from the vine, like shriveled figs from the fig tree.

Isaiah 34:4

At that time men will see the Son of Man coming in clouds with great power and glory. And he will send his angels and gather his elect from the four winds, from the ends of the earth to the ends of the heavens.

Mark 13:26–27

Then I looked and heard the voice of many angels, numbering thousands upon thousands, and ten thousand times ten thousand. They encircled the throne and the living creatures and the elders. In a loud voice they sang, "Worthy is the Lamb, who was slain, to receive power and wealth and wisdom and strength and honor and glory and praise!" Then I heard every creature in heaven and on earth and under the earth and on the sea, and all that is in them, singing: "To him who sits on the throne and to the Lamb be praise and honor and glory and power for ever and ever!"

Revelation 5:11–13

Therefore my heart is glad and my tongue rejoices; my body also will rest secure, because you will not abandon me to the grave, nor will you let your Holy One see decay. You have made known to me the path of life; you will fill me with joy in your presence, with eternal pleasures at your right hand.

Psalm 16:9–11

SUNDAY, NOVEMBER 17 A good worship service, a hard worship service. Truth. What a galvanizing force it is, what a bracing wake-up! One of my life's greatest blessings has been listening to Jack's sermons year after year after year, hearing God's truth. Such an odd process: God's Word brought forth clearly through an imperfect person whose own life is in process. Immature sermons and maturing sermons and mature sermons.

In today's sermon about God's providence, based on questions and answers 27 and 28 of the Heidelberg Catechism, Jack compared the confession of Hannah, the mother of the prophet Samuel, with that of Friedrich Nietzsche ("God is dead"), about the worlds in which each of them lived, worlds separated by thousands of years but each a world of wealth and poverty, justice and cruelty, health and death, celebration and suicide. The point was that everyone has some sort of confession about his or her world, a worldview. And the Christian's worldview is shaped by a confession of the providence of God, echoing Hannah's song in 1 Samuel 2.

The sermon had to address, of course, the problem of evil and pain. Scripture references showed that sometimes God *allows* evil and sometimes he *sends* evil. But he holds on to his people in love always, and he directs all things to the goal set for them: his glory.

Then the applications. They brought moisture to the eyes of some hearers freshly aware of our personal situation, and I clenched my teeth to outwit my own tear ducts. I prayed the preacher could keep going as his voice tightened.

Truth carried him and us hearers through. Three applications:

1. *Believers must keep the cross and everyday life together.* When good things come, we can receive them from God's fatherly hand because of the grace accomplished by Christ's death on the cross. And when in pain, we can keep our eyes on the cross, seeing its demonstration of God's immeasurable love for us.

2. *Believers must look beyond their own little worlds.* We are inclined to say, "God, whatever you do, don't touch my little fiefdom!" But God does not promise continual prosperity, joy, and health. Just as parents do not love their child less when in time they let the pacifier remain lost, or the worn-out security blanket unreplaced, so God often moves his child, too, into a larger world where there is less material security and severe trials, so that he/she can discover richer forms of God's love.

3. *Believers must relate daily life to the coming of God's kingdom.* So believers can make serving the kingdom the greatest good, rather than their own happiness. Whatever happens, joy or hurt, the Christian keeps on serving God, helping his rule and his will break through in the little and big details of personal life, and in the large and small areas of life as a whole.

Truth. Steadying and exhilarating.

Mascara clumsily daubed, I relaxed into it and recommitted myself to serving God's glory, not my own. The song of response. The offering. Prayer. Doxology. Blessing. The threefold amen and turning to leave. Negotiating the long aisle with composure.

At the back a friend slipped her arm around me. The dam broke; I wept on her shoulder. Love shone from her anxious, accepting face. She said, "We know that's the way it *is,* but sometimes we just aren't there yet."

Therefore, my dear brothers, stand firm. Let nothing move you. Always give yourselves fully to the work of the Lord, because you know that your labor in the Lord is not in vain.

1 Corinthians 15:58

My heart rejoices in the LORD; in the LORD my horn is lifted high . . . There is no one holy like the LORD; there is no one besides you; there is no Rock like our God. . . . The LORD brings death and makes alive; he brings down to the grave and raises up. . . . For the foundations of the earth are the LORD'S; upon them he has set the world. He will guard the feet of his saints, but the wicked will be silenced in darkness.

1 Samuel 2:1, 2, 6, 8, 9

WEDNESDAY, NOVEMBER 20 Our faith cell group is meditating on the Book of Romans. The commitment each member makes is to read the assigned passage every day for two weeks and then meet and share reflections. The focus is not to exegete the passage (for all the group's members have done much of that during decades of biblical teaching and preaching) but with the Spirit's help to internalize the passage into one's heart.

Romans 8 is a whirlwind shaking me every day. In it the Spirit is crying, groaning, controlling, freeing, directing, desiring, leading, putting to death, and bringing alive. He seems to be a powerful wind that blows right down into a person, his blasts removing whatever inside is of sin and death, his soft gusts steering the Christian forward into productivity, his light zephyrs wooing one into closeness with an Abba God.

And if the Spirit of him who raised Jesus from the dead is living in you, he who raised Christ from the dead will also give life to your mortal bodies through his Spirit, who lives in you.

Romans 8:11

One who does not have cancer in her lungs would never think of this, but all this power and breath and animating by the Spirit connects in my mind with what I seem to be subconsciously dreading all the time: my lungs no longer able to breathe, bringing on death. These days my mind is shaping the picture of the Spirit seamlessly picking up where my wretched lungs leave off, taking over and breathing me into the next era of my life. A critic might say wryly, "Better get back to exegesis, Mirth," but I have decided that there is no harm in this image. It is congruent enough with the chapter's statement that the Spirit will resurrect the body itself at the end of time.

Will my glorified body have pristine lungs?

I weep for my body, realizing how much I love it, so unremarkable, so broken. It seems saccharine to add that the heavenly Father loves it, too. But Christianity is astonishingly body-oriented.

I consider that our present sufferings are not worth comparing with the glory that will be revealed in us. The creation waits in eager expectation for the sons of God to be revealed . . . the creation itself will be liberated from its bondage to decay and brought into the glorious freedom of the children of God . . . Not only so, but we ourselves, who have the firstfruits of the Spirit, groan inwardly as we wait eagerly for our adoption as sons, the redemption of our bodies.

Romans 8:18, 19, 21, 23

So will it be with the resurrection of the dead. The body that is sown is perishable, it is raised imperishable; it is sown in dishonor, it is raised in glory; it is sown in weakness, it is raised in power; it is sown a natural body, it is raised a spiritual body.

1 Corinthians 15:42-44

Friday, November 22 We travel to Michigan to celebrate my mother's ninetieth birthday. A son drives with us. Sitting behind him, I am astonished by his gentleness, his realness, his breadth of information and excellent word choice as we talk. From childhood this son has kept distance between himself and us, his full-tilt-toward-the-Kingdom parents. Today he joins us easily. Has he made peace with our power in his child world, with our failures, with our assumptions? As the kilometers fold upon themselves and the winter scenery streaks by, I am surprised by hidden joy.

Tonight in the glittering hotel reception room my frail mother is poised as a queen, serene and loving as a favorite aunt. Her six children know in their own shaping how she was conditioned to discount herself, to disdain the fripperies of celebration, and to be uneasy with a human's need to be noticed. But tonight she is enveloped in grace. Without hesitation she receives the love of her children, grandchildren, and great-grandchildren. She talks with each one who comes to sit beside her, including the three-year-olds, with attentive interest. I am dazzled by her.

This small woman, stylish and alert, looking about seventy-five, has lived almost the entire twentieth century. Some of her story I "know"; I also know she would not tell her story quite the way I tell and retell it to myself. She and her brother received little overt nurture from their perfectionistic mother. As a child, to warm herself emotionally, she drew close to her pastor father's kindness and religious passion as he served rural churches in Michigan, Wisconsin, and Montana. He had grown up in an orphanage in the Netherlands and had immigrated to the United States as a single man without relatives. His conversion to the Christian faith, and his studying for the ministry through the generosity of a non-believing farmer who employed him, has always been the central drama of my mother's life. She retells it often. It is our family's "on-the-road-to-Damascus" experience, and from its miracle four generations have now been drawn into the covenant of salvation.

The children of your servants will live in your presence; their descendants will be established before you.

Psalm 102:28

For you have been my hope, O Sovereign LORD, my confidence since my youth. From birth I have relied on you; you brought me forth from my mother's womb. I will ever praise you.

Psalm 71:5–6

My mother never went to high school. Yet she has savored words all her ninety years. Raising her six children, she would recite poems and songs from her school days, entrancing herself as the sentiments curved into rhyme. She left her rural home in early teens, unsuccessfully tried secretarial college and went on to shine as a salesperson in what at that time was called a dry goods store.

She was not eager to marry. My father had picked her out as "his girl" when she was fourteen and was "always around," as she said, but she held him off until she was twenty-two. Raised with biblical literalism, she believed she had to submit to a husband without argument. She followed this dictum in her marriage, and she labeled her ensuing emotions as sinful rebellion. She spoke sometimes of being a "worm" in the eyes of God, as the old hymn states, and viewed her trials as God bending her willfulness to his will. The only cognitive tool she had for deciphering life was a theology of sin, and it took a harsh toll on her spirit.

How did she live ninety years? Surviving a flu epidemic, two world wars, extreme poverty during the Great Depression, a forceful, remote husband, too many pregnancies, constant tension headaches, strong-willed children, chronic backache, never enough money?

She did it with repression, depression, grit, and faith. During my growing up, her depression got me by the throat, an implacable life-killing sufferance.

I feel a fierce love for her.

And I feel pain.

Today I understand that my temperament has had its own part in creating my experience of my mother. My intensity and forthrightness have probably been distasteful to her, causing her to guard herself from me. Perhaps I frightened her. Still I raise lament.

She emphasized the unworthiness of human beings in the sight of God, creating for me a bleak, judgmental outlook on the world. Her dismissal of emotions and accomplishments cut me off from the strongest parts of myself, preventing the development of a firm identity. Her repulsion of body-ness left me awkward and unsure, plagued by inferiority. I grieve my teenage and young adulthood, odd mix that I was of intellect, anxiety, and puritanism. I grieve my early parenting of my own children, with my eldest the most poorly served.

> Yet you brought me out of the womb; you made me trust in you even at my mother's breast. From birth I was cast upon you; from my mother's womb you have been my God.
>
> Psalm 22:9–10

How am *I* doing? Have I made peace with my mother's power in *my* child world, with her failures, her assumptions? Readying myself for this celebration, I have been praying for that peace. So, too, my faith cell group members prayed for me at our last meeting.

And now God answers this prayer! As the celebration ends with many persons creating a shared prayer, my mother raises her aged voice and prays that her children may forgive her for any obstacle that her parenting may have caused them.

It is enough.

Suddenly I feel excitement. Fairly soon I and my mother will be together—in heaven! She will be perfect, truly a queen; and finally I will be grown up, a queen, too, washed sweet from the sour hoarding of my own and some other of my siblings' childhood pain. We will love each other with deep joy and nod to each other as we freely taste the atmosphere created by Christ's presence. The inadequacies that have slouched along through generations will be eaten up by perfect recognition of each other and by perfect regard, just as my backspace key cleanly eats up a mis-wrought sentence or shabby paragraph. My mother's father will be there and her mother . . .

And—my children?

There are more amends that I have to make.

Please, God, let them be there.

And I heard a loud voice from the throne saying, "Now the dwelling of God is with men, and he will live with them. They will be his people, and God himself will be with them and be their God. He will wipe away every tear from their eyes. There will be no more death or mourning or crying or pain, for the old order of things has passed away." He who was seated on the throne said, "I am making everything new!"

Revelation 21:3–5

No longer will there be any curse. The throne of God and of the Lamb will be in the city, and his servants will serve him. They will see his face, and his name will be on their foreheads. There will be no more night. They will not need the light of a lamp or the light of the sun, for the Lord God will give them light. And they will reign for ever and ever.

Revelation 22:3–5

December

TUESDAY, DECEMBER 3 I have so much time now, not working. The house is decorated, and it's only the first week of December. Today we got the ladder from the garage and hung the nativity banner in the stairwell. It is pieced together like a stained glass window, and when its rich velvets shake down against the wall, Advent comes to the house.

Each Christmas I make contact with a husk of puritanism left over from my early life. No Christmas tree. I was taught that a Christmas tree was a pagan thing; and, being very moralistic, I did not develop with my own children the traditions around a tree that other families have. I have felt forlorn in later years that now there is no place in my heart for one, no mystique, no delight. But there are garlands for the mantel, the sills, the railing, with baubles and lights enough.

How silly the legalistic mind is!

I feel anomie, placing things about. Unsettled, alienated. I should be prizing this special time (how many more Christmases will I have?), but its trappings seem childish to me, compared to the realness of eternity: take-charge, powerful angels instead of this brass one holding a candle; multitudes casting their crowns before God instead of these tiny carolers showered by snowflakes when their small glass world is tipped; jasper and carnelian and pearl instead of a plaid-ribboned wreath above the fireplace. Christmas is cozy and sprightly. Christ is enormous and terrifying.

Fall on your knees.

How kind God was to come to us as a baby. Nonthreatening. And we are all babies in the way we celebrate his being born. We have gotten in the habit of mixing in red bows and toys with cosmic salvation history. Christmas trees, too. Yet, despite my anomie, I will fervently "do Christmas" with my family this year, with all our traditions, special meals, gifts. For we are in earthly mode, and this is what we limited human beings do.

Come, Lord Jesus.

On coming to the house, they saw the child with his mother Mary, and they bowed down and worshiped him. Then they opened their treasures and presented him with gifts of gold and of incense and of myrrh.

Matthew 2:11

Tuesday, December 10 It's not the *Messiah* carrying me along this month, but the *Elijah.* A concert rediscovered it to us a few weeks ago. The mezzo-soprano's air, "O rest in the Lord, wait patiently for him," was sung so tenderly that my tears dripped in the darkness. (Grief as usual dribbling itself about, a snot-nosed child.)

I play the two discs over and over, usually when I am alone in the house, working in the kitchen. I crank up the volume, so that, rolling out pie crust, I am at the same time standing in the middle of the chorus or next to a soloist. Technology creates odd juxtapositions; sorry, Mendelssohn, but I am glad I do not have to wait for actual performances in order to be lifted into the drama of Baal over against God.

Crying out—and getting an answer. That is the essential back and forth of the oratorio. The rending cry: "O God of Abraham, Isaac, and Israel" answered by "Be not afraid, be not afraid, be not afraid, thus saith your God." The single voice's plaint, the choral pleading, then a piling up of reassurance, voices higher and higher.

Hey, give me that surround sound. I can relate.

Jack enters the kitchen, sees the floury counter and my apron. He hesitates, fights a wince of feeling, then says, "I will learn how to make the special pies."

> *So do not fear, for I am with you; do not be dismayed, for I am your God. I will strengthen you and help you; I will uphold you with my righteous right hand.*
>
> *Isaiah 41:10*

THURSDAY, DECEMBER 12 It's time to respond with a holiday greeting to all who have sent supportive mail and made phone calls. I gather all the addresses. An enormous, invisible ballast of prayer looms before me, with which these persons have been filling our environment the last months. It's like Lewis's Narnia world—a reality in and around and between material, sensory reality, anchoring us in love and faith, catching us up in an interplay of eternal verities. "Peter" and "Lucy," "Eustace" and "the magician's nephew"—I mean, *all my friends*—joining hands and working out eternal dramas, the drama of death and life.

May the LORD answer you when you are in distress; may the name of the God of Jacob protect you. May he send you help from the sanctuary and grant you support from Zion. May he remember all your sacrifices and accept your burnt offerings. May he give you the desire of your heart and make all your plans succeed. We will shout for joy when you are victorious and will lift up our banners in the name of our God. May the LORD grant all your requests.

Psalm 20:1–5

MONDAY, DECEMBER 16 To deepen the observance of Advent for each of us, the twelve members of my faith cell group have chosen to meditate for two weeks on Hannah's song in 1 Samuel 2 and on Mary's song in Luke 1, which echoes it.

I read them each day and keep gravitating to Hannah's. The robustness of her relish of God's power pulses from the page, like the throb you sometimes hear from the car waiting beside you at a red light. She sings a swath through the miseries of life—infertility, poverty, hunger, war, death—and then she boasts. Her boasts sound like the roar of a rock face breaking free and crashing into the sea. God—the Rock—thunders. He shatters. He creates fecundity. He shapes foundations. He breaks weapons. He turns the status quo on its head, punishing and restoring. Hannah's words soar and genuflect with a joy that is almost glee.

Hannah concludes her song by looking ahead to the advent of a king. I know this king to be David, because I live in the New Testament era. David, in turn, prefigures the advent of THE King, Jesus Christ. So this is a good selection for Advent, right?

But it's that power I want! I skitter past the king part and gaze hungrily at the words about God's power. I want God to heal me from my disease. He can do it.

Is this a legitimate way to use the Bible? I think about this, too, when I read the Psalms, whose situations usually include enemies, plotters, mockers, who are besieging the poet, and who challenge God's plan, his king, his laws. The same opponents Hannah sings about. While my only enemies are cancer cells, mindlessly doing their cannibal thing.

In my prayer journal I write a paraphrase of the first five verses of Hannah's song, tailored to my life.

My heart is filled with gladness as I come to the Lord.
In him my defenses are powerful and ready.
I dare defy cancer.
You, God, can heal me!
You are like no other person or power.
You are yourself, God alone.
You are solid, foundational, a rock.
Human wisdom can predict and plan—
That's arrogance, hubris.
You have all the knowledge about me,
You know everything that I think and do.
The cancer's evil power falters and dies.
The healthy cells recover and multiply.
My hunger for life with my loved ones is satisfied;
My life bears fruit in many ways.

Well?

It's an okay exercise, I guess. But, doing it, I realize that God answered a woman's plea for a child and a psalm-writing king's call for safety and then preserved the record of these persons' experiences through millenniums because they reveal him to be a saving God. And I do not need recovery from cancer to see God as a saving God. Much as God grieves my illness, he does not need to cure me to show me who he is. He has given me Christ.

I turn the page of my paraphrase and move on. To Mary's song and Advent, after all.

But we see Jesus, who was made a little lower than the angels, now crowned with glory and honor because he suffered death, so that by the grace of God he might taste death for everyone.

Hebrews 2:9

But . . . heal me, Lord, *heal* me. I *beseech* you.

January

FRIDAY, JANUARY 3 Year endings and year beginnings cast my mind toward big chunks of time. The newspaper sweeps up data from every sphere of life, mounding the trends and trivia under clever headlines. Then swooshes forward toward the millennium.

I face the ending of *my* allotment of time and fight to keep *my* view. I visualize the new year as a box of kitchen matches, 365 days rattling separate to the shake, each tipped to blaze with its own fire. Live one day at a time. (And make it a masterpiece.)

But, absent during the month of pleasurable holiday preparations, a fevered maudlin self-pity now whimpers again: Why is my life being wrenched about instead of being energized by clients, committees, causes; instead of cheering others on; instead of earning money and deciding how to use it? Why must I spend the days of this new year documenting an ordinary human struggle . . . that I find so extraordinary? I doubt the value of documenting it. Part of me is puckering with distaste; it is all rancid narcissism.

So I imagine working full-time again, using my remaining days for doing psychotherapy. And the spirit balks. No. To handle this piece of living I must scour my *own* inner space, sweep it bare, bone-clean. I don't know why. This insistent inner agenda embarrasses me. I read of others: "She worked until the end," "He filled his last year with tireless industry for his life cause," et cetera.

But perhaps my life's cause has been understanding the human spirit. And once again, as it was many years ago when I slogged through personal therapy, the spirit I must now understand is my own. I must watch it stutter and soar, flail and steady.

What is its value? What is the value of a human being to God? What is my value to God? What is the value of human process, intrapsychic process, at that?

A common proverb in my childhood home was "it matters not." Events, emotions, intentions didn't matter. Learn, child, that your spirit doesn't matter. The "you-ness of you" doesn't matter. Beliefs matter. Believe that you are sinful and that God accepts you because Christ died for your sins. Over against God, you are nothing. So expect nothing, other than being saved from hell. Only believe.

Half of my life, I did that. The other half . . . well, I haven't.

Just the opposite. I came to believe instead that God, a Trinity of persons in seamless, joyous fellowship, delighted in making persons with thoughts and emotions and intentions and talents, each person a unique creation, treasured in the fashioning. I came to understand that it is precisely through a child's receiving respectful attention for her thoughts and feelings that she will come to develop a sense of self, a self that can live in relationship with God and be offered to God. I came to believe that all aspects of a person are valued by God because he designed them to cohere and define humanness. I came to believe that the smallest impulse of thought or feeling has significance, just as the smallest unit of matter, a quark, is worth study.

Now this struggle to accept terminal illness. Does it matter?

I pray about it, asking God whether it matters, and it seems that God "answers" me. He brings to my mind the thought that dying is the biggest change that I will ever make and that this "getting ready to pass over" time may be the richest period of my life. He reminds me that earthly life is very important, *and* (not *but*) the perfect life with God following it is important beyond the grasping of it. I'm hanging between what is important and what is IMPORTANT, like a tightrope walker above the Niagara gorge. It is impossible for me not to notice. I need to step with intentionality—although another person may not.

Perhaps my psyche is doing what that of an eighty-year-old man or woman does while he or she walks, rocks, and naps in slowed-down time. I saw my father doing that during the last years of his life, when he was often withdrawn into a private world—a privacy he would enhance by turning off his hearing aid. My mother tells that once in rare self-disclosure he told her that he was reflecting, remembering, offering thanks, worshipping . . . and anticipating. Certainly talking and eating engaged him very little. During his last illness he refused to eat at all, although no physical obstacles to his doing so existed. Without words he enacted his determination to move forward—into the IMPORTANT.

God moves my hand toward a favorite book on my desk that has just been returned from a borrowing: *Celebration of Discipline* by Richard Foster. I idly reread the chapter on meditation. My spirit quiets with comprehension: God right now is revealing to me my task this new year.

It is to love God more than I love Jack.

I must move more intentionally toward the IMPORTANT. I've been clinging and believing and trusting and groaning and bargaining . . . all natural and necessary because of the helplessness engendered by pain. Now I must start loving. In the right order. It must become an activity, not an ideal, not a sudden switch that will happen when I am perfect, in heaven. The loving must be now.

The first months, when levels of my consciousness, unasked, would throw up pictures of Jack living after my death, I would see him ripped in half, bleeding. The pictures changed as the months went on: I often saw him muted, following routines, waiting out the time. More recently the spontaneous visions show him healed, using his gifts, nourished by loving his children and grandchildren, savoring life.

Perhaps I am ready now to give myself to loving God more than I love him. Perhaps my own grief is healing, even though I cry as I write. Why the crying? It feels as if God is asking me to bring a sacrifice, the sacrifice of Jack's privileged place in my heart. I've been reading the Book of Hebrews and its "by faith's." "By faith Abraham, when God tested him, offered Isaac as a sacrifice. He who had received the promises was about to sacrifice his one and only son, even though God had said to him, 'It is through Isaac that your offspring will be reckoned.' Abraham reasoned that God could raise the dead, and figuratively speaking, he did receive Isaac back from death" (Heb. 11:17–19). My life has no cosmic covenantal importance; my sacrifice is a fingernail sliver compared to Abraham's, but it seems to me that the faith asked is the same.

All these people were still living by faith when they died. They did not receive the things promised; they only saw them and welcomed them from a distance. And they admitted that they were aliens and strangers on earth. People who say such things show that they are looking for a country of their own. If they had been thinking of the country they had left, they would have had opportunity to return. Instead, they were longing for a better country—a heavenly one. Therefore God is not ashamed to be called their God, for he has prepared a city for them.

Hebrews 11:13–16

It is that longing that faith must now graft onto my own life, onto its sturdy lust for what is earthly. How can I long for a heavenly country if I do not spend time meditating upon its existence? How can I long for God if I do not, for lengths of time, gaze upon his beauty? He can be the most important focus of my limited capacity for love only if I increase my devotion and meditation time. Perhaps I do not need to sacrifice the privileged place of my partner in my heart but instead shift it slightly and make room for *THE* PRIVILEGED ONE.

My soul is weary with sorrow; strengthen me according to your word . . . I have chosen the way of truth; I have set my heart on your laws. . . . I run in the path of your commands, for you have set my heart free.

Psalm 119:28, 30, 32

Holy Spirit, work your rearranging in me. I long for new longing, the longing of the saints you describe in the Book of Hebrews. The longing of Psalm 42's thirsty deer. I want to pant for eternal life.

As the deer pants for streams of water, so my soul pants for you, O God. My soul thirsts for God, for the living God. When can I go and meet with God?

Psalm 42:1–2

I will sing to the LORD all my life; I will sing praise to my God as long as I live. May my meditation be pleasing to him, as I rejoice in the LORD.

Psalm 104:33–34

TUESDAY, JANUARY 7 Putting away Christmas decorations a few days ago I came upon a box of baby clothes. Although the box has been handled each time we moved, I have never been able to give its contents to a young family or to Goodwill. I have kept pushing this box to the back of a closet, letting it exist, as far as my cognizance has been concerned, for a few moments, perhaps, within each decade. My grandchildren were not able to wear these little things, for each, when adopted, were several months old.

I have to do something with this box now, or after my death my children will find the jumble inside. They will wonder, why these flannel kimonos, obviously homemade, stained at their necks by formula? this smocked dress and its slip? these very small boys' things, some with plasticized linings that pre-date the disposable diaper era? Some items are obviously baptism clothes: a tiny white dress, white suit, white bonnet and sweater, a shawl.

I shake them out onto the bed. My eyes cast about for some escape from the fact that this small heap has no importance to anyone but me. I tidy odds and ends in the room, giving the clothing only the corner of my eye. My mother made those kimonos. Now they are just rags, really, soft-washed flannel for dusting. Probably a woman needing clothes for her infant would not even pick them from the piles at the Goodwill store. But through their making, my mother reached out to her first grandchild, and so to me, with a tenderness that had not been possible before.

Why did I always push the box to the back of the closet? I recognize now that I've always resisted facing that certain experiences are over. These small suits and dresses nestle the feather heft of newborns into my arms, they shadow-joy the muscles of my shoulders, arms, and hands with the movements of feeding, bathing, dressing. My brain could always replay this sensorium when I handled these garments, although I rarely allowed it. My brain has been steadfast in its witness to the past even while guarding me from its bittersweet. My brain is going to die.

I am torn up because the value of a piece of cloth will die when my brain does? Yes.

I journal in prayer about it. The Spirit reminds me: "Not the baptism clothes, Mirth, but the baptism promise: 'I will be God to your child.'" (Forgive me, Lord! Forgive my focus on a *dress!* Forgive me. And thank you for the evidences I see of that promise, of my children's love for you.) "You have exceptional difficulty in detaching from time and things. How good it is for those of your kind that I am First and Last, Alpha and Omega, who sees your birth, your death, your floundering, your maturing, your earthbound life, and your eternity life all in one vision. I hold all this within myself always, 'remembering' it in your time language, but really simply knowing you and yours fully. My knowing will never die."

God lifted my sorrow from those pieces of cloth. I washed them, packed up most for Goodwill, and tissue-wrapped the baptismal clothes for keeping. By me, then by

Jack, perhaps later by my daughter . . . but down the years they may find their way into crates packed for children overseas . . . or be laid out with old linens in an antique shop . . . I let them go.

"In the beginning you laid the foundations of the earth, and the heavens are the work of your hands. They will perish, but you remain; they will all wear out like a garment. Like clothing you will change them and they will be discarded. But you remain the same, and your years will never end. The children of your servants will live in your presence; their descendants will be established before you."

Psalm 102:25–28

FRIDAY, JANUARY 24 A week ago we saw the movie *The English Patient.* I was eager, having read the book twice. Its five divergent characters bear forward an antiwar lament written in luminous, tactile, fragrant prose that is by turns terse and free-flowing as water. I have never before in literature met someone like the sapper, the Sikh soldier in the British army whose assignment is to dismantle land mines. Or felt such a build-up of tension as I did reading about his delicate exploration of a mine whose wires are once again cunningly connected in a new way by the enemy, wires that can blow him up in an instant. He goes crazy when the U.S. bombs Japan.

I was not prepared. The tears coursed silently; in the darkened theater no one noticed. The movie is not a good choice for anyone with diseased lungs. The English patient's burned lungs rasp throughout the sound track. Not a good choice for a person facing the ending of an intense love. One scene shows Count Alsmay curved in grief around the back of his dead lover—now an exceptionally beautiful corpse. Their reckless love affair was not what had engaged me in the reading; its flashbacks had simply provided a counterpoint of mythic attraction to the war's seared aftermath. I should have been prepared; I had read Michael Ondaatje's summing up of the process that transmutes a book into film: "A movie has its own DNA."

I read the book a third time to get *the book* back and found a sentence that fell into my heart like a polished sphere into a nest of batten. The patient, always talking, is recounting Florentine history to his young nurse, describing events from the time of Savonarola, whose pre-Reformational preaching incited his hearers to make huge bonfires of books and maps. Among his converts was Pico della Mirandola. Writes Ondaatje, "Pico down there somewhere as well, in his grey cell, watching everything with the third eye of salvation."

"With the third eye of salvation." I seize upon it, for it describes my own process. What a glory it is shedding on my way, this third eye of salvation! This writing lets me see with an additional eye. My misery at being mortal repeatedly gets reframed by seeing mortality with the eye of God's salvation. Not natural eyesight—it is a supernatural eye, a *third* eye embedded in my being by the Holy Spirit. Is it in my forehead like a Cyclopean eye? Is it strapped on like a miner's lamp? Is it in my heart, at my core?

It probably is the Holy Spirit himself.

Simeon took him in his arms and praised God, saying: "Sovereign Lord, as you have promised, you now dismiss your servant in peace. For my eyes have seen your salvation, which you have prepared in the sight of all people, a light for revelation to the Gentiles and for glory to your people Israel"

Luke 2:28–32

"What do you want me to do for you?" Jesus asked him. The blind man said, "Rabbi, I want to see." "Go," said Jesus, "your faith has healed you." Immediately he received his sight and followed Jesus along the road.

Mark 10:51–52

I pray also that the eyes of your heart may be enlightened in order that you may know the hope to which he has called you, the riches of his glorious inheritance in the saints, and his incomparably great power for us who believe.

Ephesians 1:18–19

Thursday, January 30 Lately I have been meditating on the conforming of myself to the likeness of Christ. This is a new idea for me. I have pictured myself freed from my terribly idolatrous reversal of the first commandment, my reversal of who comes first. I have pictured myself washed from my sinful deeds and thoughts. But this being made like Christ I haven't thought of at all. The fact of it fills in a missing piece of my purview.

I'm beginning to see that what has been unnerving me about being in the next life with God is the expectation that it will just be "me" who is taken to be there, perfected, to be sure, forgiven, to be sure, but still me as I know myself to be. But to be conformed to the likeness of Christ I will have to experience a transforming moment that turns me into someone different from who I am now, an expanded being, someone beautiful, someone radiant with the joy of being in relationship with God.

This is starting to greatly comfort me. It calms me. Just the knowing that I would be forgiven and free from sin didn't give me the confidence to contemplate life with God. But I now can trust that I will be somehow fleshed out, or remolded, or amplified. Perhaps my worried squirming about seeing God face-to-face has been right on all along. *I* cannot handle it, *I* am just not up to it. But my transformed self will be designed for fellowship with God. "I declare to you, brothers, that flesh and blood cannot inherit the kingdom of God, nor does the perishable inherit the imperishable. Listen, I tell you a mystery: We will not all sleep, but we will all be changed—in a flash, in the twinkling of an eye, at the last trumpet. For the trumpet will sound, the dead will be raised imperishable, and we will be changed. For the perishable must clothe itself with the imperishable, and the mortal with immortality" (1 Cor. 15:50–53).

And just as we have borne the likeness of the earthly man, so shall we bear the likeness of the man from heaven.

1 Corinthians 15:49

Dear friends, now we are children of God, and what we will be has not yet been made known. But we know that when he appears, we shall be like him, for we shall see him as he is. Everyone who has this hope in him purifies himself, just as he is pure.

1 John 3:2–3

Friday, January 31 Two persons in their seventies who are members of our church are dying, after long illnesses. I accompanied Jack in his capacity as pastor to the hospital today to visit one of them; he was unconscious and breathing with great difficulty. My presence was unimportant; but I did touch his hand and whispered good-bye. I have had a from-a-distance affection for this person ever since becoming part of this local church, for he, like myself and some others, would often raise his hands in praise as he was singing. I loved him for that.

This sad visit has comforted me. I see with certainty that death can be a beautiful release. I look ahead and see *my* death as a beautiful release. I imagine my family around me, waiting, longing with all their hearts . . . for my *release.* The balance of life and death changing, with death becoming desirable. I *know* that now. At the end the best that can happen is death. I will want it and my loved ones will want it. We will not be torn away from each other; we will willingly let each other go.

The sad visit also did the opposite—it stunned me with my own very-much-aliveness. I remember the words of the social worker at Princess Margaret Hospital last May: *"You are not dying. Dying is something quite different."* Dying is the ebbing away of all physical process. By contrast, grieving the incurable nature of one's illness, bearing the flat-out fatigue of chemotherapy, hating the irksome anger and the out-of-sorts stuff is . . . *living.* Walking in the valley of the shadow of death is . . . *living.* What I am documenting in this journal is *living,* and most people are called upon to do a chunk of this type of living.

Even though I walk through the valley of the shadow of death, I will fear no evil, for you are with me; your rod and your staff, they comfort me.

Psalm 23:4

February

Tuesday, February 4 Expecting the appointment to be routine, I go alone to meet with the oncologist today. The six chemo treatments are finished. My body is now on its own, without the protection of detective poison flushing through its tissue, blood, and bone. I picture the shrunken cancer spots as fires almost-spent, blackened and quiescent . . . an ember or two smoldering at the center. My immune system must do battle with these embers, and I will keep it so stuffed with nutrients, vitamins, and minerals that its surge will douse them dead. That is the plan.

"How big are the spots now?" I ask the oncologist. "Are they about the size they were when they were discovered last April?"

"Let me get you the official report," she offers, dashing out and returning with the computer printout. It is three sentences long. It states that there are no spots; no tumors are visible. There is only scar tissue. There are no metastases.

No tumors? *No fires at all?* I cannot quite take it in. "Is this . . . remission?"

"What we are finding out," she answers, "is that you are exceptionally sensitive to chemotherapy." *What about all the prayer? What about the health food?* "Cancer cells remain in your body but in amounts that are too small to be detected. You will probably be fine for many, many months, and then, if necessary, we will use chemotherapy again."

I am blanking out a bit. For now the spots are gone. This is THE miracle. This means TIME. And maybe . . . since the diet regimen has helped me so powerfully, there is just the tiniest chance that it can keep those microscopic cancer cells from reproducing and congealing into killer masses. In my imagination the fire-and-ember picture changes into one of soft white ash sites. Sifted cool and clean.

Like an automaton, I dress, take the elevator down, leave the hospital and walk the lengthy distance to the car. It seems that I reach it in a moment. Lines of the versified psalm are lilting themselves over and over in my head:

What shall I render to the Lord
for all his benefits to me,
How shall my soul, by grace restored
give worthy thanks, O God, to thee?

I have to tell someone. Next to the health food store, which is to be my next stop, is the hairdresser's shop where a friend works; I want to rush in and whisper in her ear, although she is probably smocked and rubber-gloved, gucking up the roots of someone's hair. No, that would not be fair, so I bubble to the server in the health store about the miracle report. She beams. Her mother has cancer, she says; what remedies have I been using? I burble on.

The car floats home. I rush into Jack's study. He is stunned, finds my news hard to take in. We keep saying to each other, "Of course there is still cancer in the system, of course it will come back," but then, gleefully, "but for *now* . . . !" We keep tripping over caution and pitching forward into elation. My eyes feel larger; relief floods foreign within me against the months of facing dying. I laugh to my children on the phone: "It's taken me nine months to come to accept that I will be leaving this life soon, but only three hours to adjust to the possibility that I may be living longer!"

What will happen now? Will I splash about in the relief like a fool, forgetting that the passing-over process is just being drawn out? Will I lose my longing to long for seeing God?

> *Praise the LORD, O my soul; all my inmost being, praise his holy name. Praise the LORD, O my soul, and forget not all his benefits. He forgives all my sins and heals all my diseases; he redeems my life from the pit and crowns me with love and compassion. He satisfies my desires with good things, so that my youth is renewed like the eagle's.*
>
> Psalm 103:1–5

WEDNESDAY, FEBRUARY 5 The funeral today. Attending many funerals in the congregations of which I have been a part, more often than not I have become tearful at some point in the service, imaginatively entering into the grief process of the persons bereft. Today, no tears. Instead, hyper-alertness to each spoken and sung word, a radar scan for truth for myself and for all of us attending. Perhaps the wrestling of these months has made death as matter-of-fact as life to me, while before it was an aberration.

My eyes raised themselves again and again to what I love best about this church: the very large round window high above the pulpit, fronted by an enormous wood and brass cross. The cross's arms extend beyond the window's round edge, and its main beam extends above and far below that edge. The window's many-faceted stained glass shapes of silver grey, pearl, beige, and gold geometrically ring the center of the cross, diffusing light that is at times soft, at times brilliant.

Worshipping in this church the last years I have often seen this window as a representation of the glorified Christ, visible to believers through the cross. Or I have thought of the window as the opening of Christ's tomb, speared with glittering angels. Today the window became the entrance to Paradise, its cross the door and its radiant depths an endlessly opening up terrain. I "saw" my friend cavorting far behind and beyond the cross, hale, free, at play in the garden of God's presence.

Therefore Jesus said again, "I tell you the truth, I am the gate for the sheep. . . . I am the gate; whoever enters through me will be saved. He will come in and go out, and find pasture. . . . I have come that they may have life, and have it to the full."

John 10:7, 9–10

Then the righteous will shine like the sun in the Kingdom of their Father.

Matthew 13:43

When he has brought out all his own, he goes on ahead of them, and his sheep follow him because they know his voice.

John 10:4

SUNDAY, FEBRUARY 9 Because so many persons have been supporting me with ongoing prayer and with cards slipped into our church mail slot, I want to tell them the news myself, rather than have it printed in the bulletin. When I visualize my doing so, I see myself animated and upbeat, exultantly praising God. But standing in front of the congregation, saying my piece, my voice is quiet and, once, almost breaks. The congregation sits stolidly when I have finished; then pours its joy into lustily singing the song I request, "What shall I render to the Lord?"

How can I repay the LORD for all his goodness to me? I will lift up the cup of salvation and call on the name of the LORD. I will fulfill my vows to the LORD in the presence of all his people.

Psalm 116:12-14

Later, many are ashamed of their silence. At least ten persons tell me, "I wanted to say aloud, 'Praise God!' or applaud." We nod ruefully that our worship tradition does not encourage such spontaneity. "Well, we are able to praise God one-to-one, anyway," I reassure them. "And many *wanted* to respond right at the moment. We're making progress." For a split second I see each person in this Sunday crowd transformed, radiant with the likeness of Christ, totally absorbed in moment-to-moment praising of him. This happy after-service coffee time, the hugs given me, and the beaming smiles are pale hints of behaviors in our coming life together that will . . . knock the socks off us all! To my astonishment, I momentarily feel a deep, true eagerness for that life.

TUESDAY, FEBRUARY 18 Two weeks after the wonderful news of the tumors' disappearance, pain is back. I ignore it. Then I face it: It is because of the skiing motions of the NordicTrack™, I tell myself; it is because I stretched my arm wide, mopping the floor. But yesterday there was more than the armpit pain attributable to exercise; as I sat quietly this morning with a client, pain in the upper right chest area pulsed softly for a few moments, stopped, returned, stopped, returned.

Conclusions jump up. First, that power diet apparently is not going to overbalance the cancer. Secondly, that X ray must not have been sufficiently exact; perhaps a CAT scan would have shown something. Thirdly, our personal time moves into fast forward again, terribly precious, its everyday joys *vibrating.* I now feel profound embarrassment about having widely shared my good news. As someone said to my daughter, "There is no greater excitement than being in the middle of answered prayer!" For two weeks I've been the focus of that excitement, receiving cards and flowers again, each sender jubilant about God's kindness, exulting in the miracle of the scar-tissued lungs. I've been pulling lots of persons along on this roller-coaster ride. The recurrence of pain humiliates me before them.

But I notice that in my deep disappointment there is also calm. The tears come, but I can stop them, too, when enough is enough. Imagining cancer's quick ravage is not clawing me into pieces as it did when I heard the diagnosis last April. The lengthened daily worship and this writing, seemingly so narcissistic, have done their work—readying me for passing over into eternity. I want very much to stretch out the time I have with Jack, *and* . . . my inner eye sparkles at the thought of being conformed to the likeness of Christ, flourishing within his brilliant presence. The prize Paul wrote about running toward has become desirable, as it was not last May. That cruel choice—life with Jack or full communion with God—no longer seems cruel; the two concepts do not even present themselves as a choice. Now I expect that the one will flow into the other; the Holy Spirit has truly taught me that in heaven Jack and I will have a relationship so unimaginably splendored that I might as well give up the imagining and simply trust. What we have now is the firstfruits—but, oh, the harvest!

I call the oncologist. Because of a cancellation I can see her today. Her probing fingers discover nothing unusual. Another X ray is scheduled and, because commitments prevent me from seeing her for a week, I decide to wait that long to find out the results.

I want a few days of calm before the storm.

On the appointment day my oncologist's colleague tells us the results, since she is away: "The lungs are clear," adding, "but if you are continuing to have discomfort, we'd better do a CAT scan."

March

Saturday, March 1 The pain is not increasing. I can plausibly attribute almost all of it to the exercise of my arm. I felt cheerful during the CAT scan two days ago, performed by two soft-spoken doctors. Of course, the usual problem of finding a vein in which to inject the dye caused them frustration. After five stabs, they called in an emergency ward nurse, who warmed my arm with a heated towel and successfully jabbed in the shunt.

I'm believing "the miracle" again, on the basis of that second "all clear" X ray. A carefree mood has settled in, a very familiar mood, although I would not have remembered it; it's the mood of my cancer-free days, my everyday mood of a year ago, so long ago. *I would not have remembered it*. I feel young, light, playful; the future stretches out—one example: Because of the joy my daily Bible reading gives me, the plan forms in me to become a trained Bethel Bible Series teacher once Jack has retired. The surge of energy I feel is astonishing; a high tide of possibilities rushes through me; it lifts me up; I sense that I have much good work yet to do!

Having dinner with friends, they share that one of them is being tested for cancer. And after a few days we learn that cancer is indeed present. I keep thinking of them, mourning for them, knowing that a shadow will now dreary their every day, their nights, their future. But personally I feel that I am in a different place. I stand somewhat apart from these friends, not shoulder to shoulder in the same strait. I have already distanced myself from my own cancer; unconsciously I have been placing myself in the category of "cured," the category of those who have received a miracle.

My mind—the startling speed with which it leaps hurdles of realism and caution, dashing headlong into assumptions of health—dumbfounds me.

He will call upon me, and I will answer him; I will be with him in trouble, I will deliver him and honor him. With long life will I satisfy him and show him my salvation.

Psalm 91:15-16

THURSDAY, MARCH 6 This afternoon we received the results of the CAT scan. I went to the appointment optimistic; Jack went, wary. Today she was matter-of-fact. Scanned by technology more sophisticated than the X ray, the old tumor sites show themselves not to be absent but to be "stable." As well, there is a new nodule of cancer, hardly a centimeter in size, on the right lung.

In torturous slow motion her words shake themselves down into our comprehension, while at the same time searing our brains with lightning-quick understanding. *(1) New cancer has started already, with the chemo treatments stopped for barely two months. (2) The power food is a false hope, no match for the cancer's stealth.*

She emphasizes how small the nodule is. "So it's not time to start chemo again?" "Oh, no, we must save that . . . but of course chemo won't be able to hold back the cancer forever . . ." *I am yelling inside: My cure, my miracle, where has it gone, were we so stupid, two X rays were clear, we trusted that, God, you must have wanted us to know this, otherwise we would have been in bliss until the new spot was large enough to show on an X ray, God, you planned this scan, you wanted us to know . . . you wanted us to know this . . . you wanted us to know . . .*

She suggests I try a new hormonal drug in tablet form, Arimidex, that has just been released for use in Canada. Possibly it may shrink the new spot. Our solemn agreement covers the stony daze we are in.

Tonight I crept into God's presence. I cried a lot, which I haven't done for a long time. I worshipped. I felt God's Abba-love around me and his Spirit within me. I accepted that my road ahead will be the same as it is for billions of cancer patients, with no miraculous cure; instead, more debilitation, more attempts to stave the killer off, bits of respite perhaps, then more wasting and pain, and a final ravage screeching through my body, tearing it from my soul.

And then I will be with God.

That is the miracle. I *am* starting to be ready.

For you did not receive a spirit that makes you a slave again to fear, but you received the Spirit of sonship. And by him we cry, "Abba, Father." The Spirit himself testifies with our spirit that we are God's children. Now if we are children, then we are heirs—heirs of God and co-heirs with Christ, if indeed we share in his sufferings in order that we may also share in his glory.

Romans 8:15-17

I will not die but live, and will proclaim what the LORD has done. The LORD has chastened me severely, but he has not given me over to death. Open for me the gates of righteousness; I will enter and give thanks to the LORD. This is the gate of the LORD through which the righteous may enter. I will give you thanks, for you answered me; you have become my salvation.

Psalm 118:17–21

Come and listen, all you who fear God; let me tell you what he has done for me. I cried out to him with my mouth; his praise was on my tongue. If I had cherished sin in my heart, the Lord would not have listened; but God has surely listened and heard my voice in prayer. Praise be to God, who has not rejected my prayer or withheld his love from me!

Psalm 66:16–20

SATURDAY, MARCH 8 My spirit is feisty today. Nothing really has changed, I tell Jack, except that now when the new tumor eventually appears on an X ray, we will not be surprised. Until then, we can keep on enjoying this "remission." After all, we do not know how fast the cancer will grow. My energy is at a high level, vacation awaits, I'm taking a few new clients—let's run with what we have. Let's allow our children and our friends to have "the miracle." As we would be having it, but for the scan.

Jack tells me last night's dream. He had struggled and struggled to subdue a vicious dog, but it could not be controlled. Eventually it was somehow confined to the backyard, but it was still a menace, evoking everyone's uneasiness.

Yes.

My own dreams were full of excrement.

Nothing has changed? Everything has changed. No miracle. This mortal body is plagued by decay that will eat it up. Sooner rather than later. I will be with God, and Jack will be a single person, uncoupled from my love.

WEDNESDAY, MARCH 12 Last night I fought off tears in the annual Day of Prayer service, something I haven't had to do for awhile. Is Arimidex going to pitch me into depression the way Tamoxifen did? My first thought on waking was of dying. I must not let myself sink too far into depression before using an antidepressant if it's needed. I can't just stop taking this tiny pill; it is the only new weapon we have. It's going to shrink that tiny spot, right? That fiery ember? Please, God, let your angels blast into my system on the lightning bolts of this new drug. Shrivel the spot! I beseech you!

THURSDAY, MARCH 13 Along with bleak thoughts, dizziness. I hate the way these hormone preparations make my spirit crumple, with the thought "It would just be better to have this all over with" a dull refrain. All I can manage for devotions is listening to John Michael Talbot's Scripture songs, while holding my head very still. His plaintive verses cry what I have no energy to cry.

In the same way, the Spirit helps us in our weakness. We do not know what we ought to pray for, but the Spirit himself intercedes for us with groans that words cannot express. And he who searches our hearts knows the mind of the Spirit, because the Spirit intercedes for the saints in accordance with God's will.

Romans 8:26–27

Friday, March 14 I stop taking the Arimidex.

Saturday, March 15 The day has ended with heartbreak because I am envisioning my children living without me. The cause is today's visit, seeing one of them I hadn't visually seen since Christmas because of the winter's wild scourge and the two hours' distance between us. Anguish is carving me hollow today. Two of my children have had significant troubles, and always I have been their "present help." I have breathed my love fiercely before them and around them, doing battle with infirmities that might otherwise beat them down. The best that I am has been theirs for the need. *It is my task to carry them.*

I ask God's Spirit to nestle trust into my aching hollowness—trust that his judo-power will deflect the evil of my illness and death from my children and return it back to them as a deepening, beautifying force in their lives.

I know of young mothers and young fathers having cancer, dying, saying good-bye to their young children, to teens. What right have I to devastation that my adult children must live without the resource of my passion beside them? No right. And they are brave enough. It is I grieving the illusion of being indispensable. What is cutting my hands are the crumbling shards of my being their *mother.* Come . . . open your hands . . . let the pieces gently fall.

And we know that in all things God works for the good of those who love him, who have been called according to his purpose. . . . For I am convinced that neither death nor life, neither angels nor demons, neither the present nor the future, nor any powers, neither height nor depth, nor anything else in all creation, will be able to separate us from the love of God that is in Christ Jesus our Lord.

Romans 8:28, 38–39

Wednesday, March 19 I started taking the hormonal tablet once again. It is the one new hope. I am praying that I may be able to tolerate it after all.

God has given me a new tool: a schema by which the entire Bible can be read in one year. My initial exploration of the Internet was to find the web site of my denomination, and what the site offered first off was this Bible-reading plan. Two Old Testament passages and two New Testament passages each day—probably about five chapters of reading in all. My system is to read the passages, write down the verses that particularly strike me, and then write a few sentences that comment on the connection among the passages. Food for my soul!

If I live another year, I will be able to read the whole Bible with concentration. If I do not, God will turn my eyes from his self-revelation in the Bible to his dazzling revelation of himself to me in heaven. Am I blessed or am I not?

As I begin, the Deuteronomy and Joshua passages are startling in their record of the "passing over" process: the back-and-forth hesitation, the enjoinders to courage, the reluctance, the *need for faith*. The inspired record nourishes me in my situation as existentially as my health food regimen. My life too is now a going forward with God into a frightening situation. To get to the Promised Land.

For years I have neglected the Old Testament books. Through the agency of cancer, my "third eye of salvation" is now processing their record with an acuity it never had before.

. . . so is my word that goes out from my mouth: It will not return to me empty, but will accomplish what I desire and achieve the purpose for which I sent it.

Isaiah 55:11

But you have come to Mount Zion, to the heavenly Jerusalem, the city of the living God. You have come to thousands upon thousands of angels in joyful assembly, to the church of the firstborn, whose names are written in heaven. You have come to God, the judge of all men, to the spirits of righteous men made perfect, to Jesus the mediator of a new covenant, and to the sprinkled blood that speaks a better word than the blood of Abel.

Hebrews 12:22–24

TUESDAY, MARCH 25 The sweetness of bodies.

"I wonder when it will be the last time."

"We probably won't know that it *is* the last time."

The beauty of a person.

The man said, "This is now bone of my bones and flesh of my flesh; she shall be called 'woman,' for she was taken out of man." For this reason a man will leave his father and mother and be united to his wife, and they will become one flesh.

Genesis 2:23–24

THURSDAY, MARCH 27 Today I heard Dr. Mel Hugen of Calvin Seminary give two presentations to pastors and their spouses about the church's ministry to persons with same-sex attractions.

He stressed the universality of a human's longing to be fully known in relationships of intimacy. The creation structure of marriage attempts to fill this longing, he said, but really it is in union with Christ that we are fully known, and in that union we are also known to one another. This is true for married persons, and for singles and persons with same-sex attractions for whom the Lord's revealed will is celibacy.

He noted that the Bible uses the same word for "union with a marriage partner" and for "union of the church with Christ." He paraphrased Ephesians 5:32 in this way: "Now the mystery is revealed: The marriage bond is really about Christ and the church." He concluded that that is why there will be no marriage in heaven and no sexual relationships for persons with glorified bodies. The church's union will be with Christ.

Busily taking notes, I felt his words resonate within my heart, taming its struggle to find peace with separation from Jack. Calming its bewilderment about relationships in heaven. The relationship I treasure so much is just a stand-in, a glimmer of a far more satisfying relationship: union with Christ. Unbelievable, really. Earth-shattering! yes, *earth-shattering,* a breaking of a creation-mold that has cupped my earthly life.

"Husbands, love your wives, just as Christ loved the church and gave himself up for her to make her holy, cleansing her by the washing with water and through the word, and to present her to himself as a radiant church, without stain or wrinkle or any other blemish, but holy and blameless. In this same way, husbands ought to love their wives as their own bodies. He who loves his wife loves himself. After all, no one ever hated his own body, but he feeds and cares for it, just as Christ does the church—for we are members of his body. 'For this reason a man will leave his father and mother and be united to his wife, and the two will become one flesh.' This is a profound mystery—but I am talking about Christ and the church. However, each one of you also must love his wife as he loves himself, and the wife must respect her husband" (Eph. 5:25–33).

Tuesday, April 1 An embarrassment sits uneasily in me, frowning up my forehead sometimes.

I've been reading a number of books written by women who, like me, are walking breast cancer's *via dolorosa.* Several accounts are written turnabout with a partner, who then ends the story with the death of the lover, the cancer patient.

The struggle for many of us facing death is, "What happens to my Self, or to my ego, to my 'I-ness,' to my 'me' when I die?" My sisters-in-grief touch on this with varying degrees of intensity, finding useful tenets in Jungian psychology, or Eastern mysticism, or transpersonal psychology, or Judaism, to help them grapple with the question. Each believes that individual personhood ends with this life. (The Eastern mystic, of course, accepts that reincarnation is necessary for those not yet sufficiently purified to move on to a person-less existence.) These gallant women stare down the loss of the personal self, work to accept it, do accept it. Individuality is a condition from which to graduate.

Hence my embarrassment. I believe that I will live on *as a person, as myself* after my death. *My* wrestlings have been wreathed about by the Christian Scriptures, and that is what they have breathed into me. How can it be true? A personal identity beyond death? Compared to these women's moving beyond individuality, it seems so childish, so immature and egotistical. A primitive level of belief, characteristic of an earlier century, a younger stage of human faith development. The faith of a person who believes in Bible stories. Quaint.

So I scowl with uneasiness. I don't like being unsophisticated, behindhand, a bit thick.

Where is the wise man? Where is the scholar? Where is the philosopher of this age? Has not God made foolish the wisdom of the world? For since in the wisdom of God the world through its wisdom did not know him, God was pleased through the foolishness of what was preached to save those who believe. . . . For the foolishness of God is wiser than man's wisdom, and the weakness of God is stronger than man's strength

1 Corinthians 1:20–21, 25

Wednesday, April 2 I puzzle and I puzzle. Pressed to the point, I admit that I really don't have a clue how I will be myself after death. Who I will be.

But automatically I type *who* rather than *what.*

My mind—no doubt guided by the Holy Spirit—worries biblical teaching around. The central dynamic of the Bible is a heart-to-heart one: LOVE. Love requires persons. It needs subjects and objects, individuals.

God *is* love, a fellowship of three *persons* in one, not radiant mind or serene bliss. As a person himself, he creates persons in his image, loves them, chases after them when they are not interested in him, gives the life of his Son to pay for their unconscionable disinterest. After they die, he talks about them being alive, naming their personal names: Abraham, Isaac, Jacob, Moses, Elijah, the poor man Lazarus, Jesus Christ. He says, "I am not the God of the dead, but of the living."

When I think about psyche, Self, ego, soul, spirit, body, mind—I blur out, because I cannot predict how any of these concepts will exist or be rearranged or be transformed to create the new humanity that is the New Testament's hope. I know I will be transformed to be like Christ, so I will be quite different from what I am today. But I believe with all my heart that I will be myself. More truly myself than I have ever been in this life, misshapen as I am by sin.

Could this be an intimation of this changing/staying oneself—what sometimes happens to a person who experiences psychotherapeutic healing? A woman who for many years has hidden being abused often initially sits mute in the counseling sessions, her leadership gifts unknown to herself, her humor buried, her intelligence masked. Then, as recovery proceeds over many months, she unfolds like a flower, creatively loving the people in her life, participating in church and community projects, or marching off to university, her mind and wit ranging free, her eyes sparkling. Yet she is not a different person from the one who originally came for help. She is a freed-up person.

So the person transformed after death, living in perfect communion with Christ?

The more I reflect, personal identity continuing beyond the grave no longer strikes me as a quaint belief. It is a tough belief. Because getting the love part right is something no human is able to do.

"One of the teachers of the law came and heard them debating. Noticing that Jesus had given them a good answer, he asked him, 'Of all the commandments, which is the most important?' 'The most important one,' answered Jesus, 'is this: "Hear, O Israel, the Lord our God, the Lord is one. Love the Lord your God with all your heart and with all your soul and with all your mind and with all your strength"'" (Mark 12:28–30).

And it is a fearful thing to fall into the hands of a personal God. It would really be easier to no longer have a personal identity, easier not to have to meet him.

Lord Jesus, I fling myself and my embarrassment upon you. Hold on to me in this life and in my death.

For we know him who said, "It is mine to avenge; I will repay," and again, "The Lord will judge his people." It is a dreadful thing to fall into the hands of the living God.

Hebrews 10:30–31

"Now about the dead rising—have you not read in the book of Moses, in the account of the bush, how God said to him, 'I am the God of Abraham, the God of Isaac, and the God of Jacob'? He is not the God of the dead, but of the living."

Mark 12:26–27

MONDAY, APRIL 7 Some of the perspectives I meet as I read Eastern mysticism keep snagging my thoughts.

Attachment is one. Attachment is undesirable, for everything to which one is attached is an illusion. How does this fit with the Christian faith, which emphasizes the transitory nature of life?

My married and unmarried children are coming for Easter dinner this year.

I am glad that they will join in a celebration of Christ's resurrection, but my mind also revs up energy in another way around their coming. Unseemly energy, it seems to me, around a beautiful tablecloth, matched place settings, a centerpiece.

I polish the silver and think about "attachment." In ironing the long, embroidered cloth, I hang and re-hang the folds, trying once again the impossible task of getting them perfect. I handle a plate of my grandmother's dishes, so thin as to be almost translucent, edge deckled with worn gold. I worry about who will care for these dishes when I am dead.

Calling the above "attachment" is an understatement. A grasping after what is passing away. Attachment is at the root of my suffering this year, its tearing of my frantic grasp of persons to whom I am attached, its ripping away of a vision of old age to which I am attached. The large contours of my life and its smallest details keep getting scissored by relentless cutting.

But is all that to which I am attached *an illusion?*

I shriek, "I don't want to think that way!" I never had silver until we bought a set at a flea market several years ago. I never had china until I inherited my grandmother's. I never had a long table until Jack found a walnut drop-leaf one, which he refinished, and for which we had leaves made. The tablecloth, a yard sale find. I had to wait for my pretty table, my few things that are a shabby pittance compared to the truly valuable possessions that wealthy people have! I cherish them! And I want to, without apology!

There is plenty of time to shriek, to think. It's a twelve-place setting of silverplate. Will the rubbing and shining . . . of this illusion . . . ever be finished?

Heaven and earth will pass away, but my words will never pass away.

Mark 13:31

THURSDAY, APRIL 10 Quite a few years ago I saw the movie *Babette's Feast* for the first time. It stirred me more than any other movie has before or since. Because the sober Christian sect it pictures resembles in an exaggerated way the repressed Christianity of my mother, which hypnotized the first part of my life.

The irony of the film is that the prodigally lavish feast offered by French chef Babette, who has lived incognito within the sect's spare style of life for many years, dispenses more grace to its handful of elderly believers than have their years of hymn singing and bleak living. More correctly, the feast *connects* the participants with the grace that shimmers in the chalice of their beliefs and their songs. They not only sing about the New Jerusalem, they *taste* it. After the dinner, they drift homeward with arms linked, their face lines softened with love for each other.

Babette spends the entire amount she has won in a lottery to create the feast, her gift to the people who have sheltered her. She buys china and silver, and goblets of different sizes for the wines. With a stove-warmed iron she smoothes away the fold lines of the tablecloth as it lies on the table. Her cooking is a choreography of deftness, care, and pleasure. There is no hurry and no indecision. Course follows course, each matched with its wine. The feast is perfection.

She spends all she has, extends herself to the limit of what she is capable.

One of my friends, after seeing the film, said, "Christ is my Babette." Another: "It's important to celebrate special occasions with beautiful meals so that we are reminded of the joy and perfection that await us in the new heaven and the new earth."

For the Christian, I realize, the transient nature of this life does not make it an illusion. The beautiful things of life, though passing away, are valuable as a *foretaste.* Why do I always first see everything as "either/or?" My paltry treasures can dilate my eyes to see eternity.

The silver shines white, all the serving pieces, too.

Radiance.

> *In his great mercy he has given us new birth into a living hope through the resurrection of Jesus Christ from the dead, and into an inheritance that can never perish, spoil or fade—kept in heaven for you.*
>
> 1 Peter 1:3–4

Friday, April 11 Good Friday today, with its celebration of Holy Communion. This past year the celebrations of the Lord's Supper have seemed to be a reaching out from heaven to me by the glorified Jesus. A memory, perhaps, of Michelangelo's famous Sistine Chapel painting, with its reaching hands between Creator and Adam; but in the supper, I experience Jesus reaching down to me, not across. I eat and drink, served by his hands. The enactment a bridge between this life and what is to come.

> *I tell you, I will not drink of this fruit of the vine from now on until that day when I drink it anew with you in my Father's kingdom.*
>
> Matthew 26:29

Sunday, April 13 Easter. In my consciousness today the tomb seemed to gape creation-wide, swallowing the entire death-marred cosmos, of which my own mortality is an eye-speck part. The wonder still that eye-specks matter to God. That he resurrects them.

In contrast to my vision, today's celebration seemed starkly simple, even pedestrian. Old and new songs. Trumpets shaky on some of the notes. Casual joy.

One believes the miracle or one does not.

I believe it. The resurrection of Christ's body and of my body. Once again out of sync with the beliefs of many others. Most persons are eager to be done with the rotten old thing, even if that takes many reincarnations, or is accomplished by the simple breakdown of body elements into humus.

By contrast, the Christian faith is almost body-obsessed! God incarnates the second person of the Trinity, his Son, into a physical body. The *dying* of this body was crucial to his enactment of salvation: "But now he has reconciled you *by Christ's physical body* through death to present you holy in his sight, without blemish and free from accusation—" (Col. 1:22), causing Paul to conclude ". . . so that now as always Christ will be exalted *in my body,* whether by life or by death" (Phil. 1:20).

How will God resurrect bodies? Jesus' body was a scant three days in the grave, so its rejuvenation might not have been difficult. But a part of my body was already burned to ash some years ago, and after death my disease-ravaged body will decompose in its coffin. At that, it meets a gentler fate than that of the billions of bodies that are dismembered, drowned, even eaten. The gruesome, nauseous, hideousness of death. *The resurrection of the body?* Am I nuts? Festus, the governor of Caesarea in Paul's time, cried out, "You are out of your mind, Paul! . . . Your great learning is driving you insane!" (Acts 26:24) when

Paul spoke to him about Jesus, the first to rise from the dead.

It's of one piece with personhood continuing into eternity, I think. As in this life I am a unity of body and spirit, so will I be in the next. God who created everything that exists out of nothing can certainly do what my mind cannot process.

The new Christians in Corinth couldn't process it either. The Holy Spirit gives Paul words to explain it: "But someone may ask, 'How are the dead raised? With what kind of body will they come?' How foolish! What you sow does not come to life unless it dies. When you sow, you do not plant the body that will be, but just a seed, perhaps of wheat or of something else. But God gives it a body as he has determined, and to each kind of seed he gives its own body. . . . So it will be with the resurrection of the dead. The body that is sown is perishable, it is raised imperishable; it is sown in dishonor, it is raised in glory; it is sown in weakness, it is raised in power; it is sown a natural body, it is raised a spiritual body" (1 Cor. 15:35–38, 42–44).

A spiritual body.

An oxymoron? A perfect integration?

I have always loved Paul's passionate cry, "I want to know Christ and the power of his resurrection and the fellowship of sharing in his sufferings, becoming like him in his death, and so, somehow, to attain to the resurrection from the dead" (Phil. 3:10–11).

Easter.

. . . the Lord Jesus Christ, who, by the power that enables him to bring everything under his control, will transform our lowly bodies so that they will be like his glorious body.

Philippians 3:20–21

I declare to you, brothers, that flesh and blood cannot inherit the kingdom of God, nor does the perishable inherit the imperishable. Listen, I tell you a mystery: We will not all sleep, but we will all be changed—in a flash, in the twinkling of an eye, at the last trumpet. For the trumpet will sound, the dead will be raised imperishable, and we will be changed. For the perishable must clothe itself with the imperishable, and the mortal with immortality.

1 Corinthians 15:50–53

TUESDAY, APRIL 22 A year ago on this day I received the diagnosis of incurable cancer in my lungs.

How am I doing?

Slowly, with God's help, a rearranging of my inner world has occurred, tedious and irksome as this self-therapy has been for me. I don't think the anguish will ever return in the same way, or the single focus on departing.

The cancer is still not large enough to show on an X ray, thank God, although we know it awaits. I have resumed my psychotherapy practice, with my personal situation not an obstacle—in fact, it is sometimes useful, when a client deals with grief. I do not feel lonely and apart in a worship service. I look around and know that we all have an eternity of glorious life ahead of us, although most of my fellow-worshippers have their energies focused elsewhere right now.

Being with my family will never be the same; it is distilled joy. Deep sadness comes now and then, but soon the thought follows: "You've *done* that; use the time you have left for focusing on the 'now that is.'"

God is helping me to wear my mortality more lightly.

The cords of death entangled me; the torrents of destruction overwhelmed me. The cords of the grave coiled around me; the snares of death confronted me. In my distress I called to the LORD; I cried to my God for help. From his temple he heard my voice; my cry came before him, into his ears.

Psalm 18:4–6

. . . let us run with perseverance the race marked out for us. Let us fix our eyes on Jesus, the author and perfecter of our faith, who for the joy set before him endured the cross, scorning its shame, and sat down at the right hand of the throne of God.

Hebrews 12:1–2

WEDNESDAY, APRIL 30 We keep praying for time.